ANXIETY DISORDERS:
THE CAREGIVERS

D0710151

ANXIETY DISORDERS: THE CAREGIVERS

Information for Support People, Family and Friends

3rd Edition

Kenneth V. Strong

SelectBooks, Inc.

This book is dedicated to all support people
and those they support.

Anxiety Disorders: The Caregivers
©2003 Oakminster Publishing.*
Published 1996 and 1997 by Oakminster Publishing. Original
title: *Anxiety Panic Attacks and Agoraphobia. Information for
Support People, Family and Friends.*

*Oakminster Publishing is a division of Oakminster Products Incorporated.

Third Edition 2003 by SelectBooks, Inc. For information address
SelectBooks, Inc., New York, New York.

ISBN 1-59079-056-1

Library of Congress Cataloging-in-Publication Data
Strong, Kenneth V. (Kenneth Vincent), 1938–
Anxiety disorders: the caregivers: information for support people,
family and friends / Ken Strong—3rd ed.
    p. cm.
Previous editions published under title: Anxiety, panic attacks
and agoraphobia.
    Includes bibliographical references.
    ISBN 1-59079-056-1 (pbk.)
1. Anxiety—Popular works. 2. Anxiety—Patients—Home care—
Popular works. 3. Caregivers—Popular works. I. Title.
RC531.S77 2003
362.1'9685223—dc21
                    2003004537

Manufactured in the United States of America
                10 9 8 7 6 5 4 3 2 1

Contents

Preface to the Third Edition

THIS EDITION FOLLOWS THE GOALS of the previous two editions:

- to provide support people with information, guidance and suggestions on being a caregiver/support person to those with anxiety, panic attacks and/or agoraphobia.

- to provide people suffering from these illnesses a source to explain the nature of their problem without having to hand out a stack of books.

- to provide friends, family, co-workers and others with a clear concise explanation of the disorders and practical suggestions for working with these people.

Since it is possible for a person to have more than one of the anxiety disorders, or they can morph from one to another, the book has been expanded to include more of the anxiety spectrum. The major exception is separation anxiety. This topic was excluded because the many books available on separation anxiety are usually directed toward parents and the inclusion here is not necessary.

Information on medications is now widely available both on the Internet and through pharmacists. Therefore the chapter on medications gives a very brief overview of the drugs available, but concentrates on concerns that those with anxiety may have about just taking a pill.

The terms "caregivers" and "support people" are used interchangeably, but my preference is for "support people" since "caregivers" seems to be used more for terminal illnesses—which anxiety disorders are not. For the sake of clarity I have, throughout the book, adopted the use of "she" rather than continually inserting "he/she," etc.

Expanding the contents of the book necessitated changing the title from *Anxiety, Panic Attacks and Agoraphobia* to its current one.

Some professionals may take issue with the occasional latitude taken in differentiating between the individual disorders of the anxiety spectrum. For example, the strict diagnostic criteria of general anxiety disorder and anticipatory anxiety are not always as clearly differentiated as some may prefer. It was thought that presenting the information as we have is adequate for the caregiver and avoids lengthy/confusing explanations in an area which can easily morph from one to the other.

Also, the terms "counselor" and "counselling" are used in a broad manner throughout the book. Except for the sections in which types of treatment are discussed, the terms are meant to be all inclusive.

A grass roots project such as this, which is based almost entirely on input from individuals, is the product of the experiences of thousands of people. It is impossible to list them all, and most have indicated they wish to remain anonymous and wish only to see their contributions useful to others.

Having said this, there are some I can single out. They are not professionally directly responsible for the

contents but have, in one way or another, been of great
assistance:

Bronwyn Fox. Author, lecturer and director of the
Anxiety Panic Hub in South Australia. For general support and hours of discussions.
www.panicattacks.com.au

Vickie French-Lankarge. Writer. For collating and
writing the chapter on the workplace.

Kathryn I'Anson. Director, Anxiety Recovery
Centre. Victoria, Australia. For permitting us to repro-
duce a chapter from her book ...*nine, ten, do it again.
A Guide to Obsessive Compulsive Disorder.*

Dr. Stuart Shipko, M.D. Panic Disorders Institute.
Pasadena, California, USA. www.algy.com/pdi/

Dr. Ian A. Gillespie. Psychiatrist. Victoria, BC.
Canada. www.drivesafe.com

Dr. Sanjay Chugh, Senior Consultant Psychiatrist
based in New Delhi, India

April Harrington, Project Manager, Multifamily
Program Center. HUD, Oklahoma. USA

Dr. David Perry. Psychologist. University of
Westminster. London, England.

Dr. Andjelka Stones-Abbasi. Psychologist formerly
with the University of Westminster, London, England
and now co-founder of the Global Egg Donation
Resource.

Introduction

A LL THOSE WHO SUFFER from anxiety illnesses are no
doubt pleased to see that the medical community is
now much more aware of these illnesses, and that effective treatment is more readily available. Progress has
also been seen in the general public's attitude toward
anxiety disorders, making it more acceptable to admit
to having problems with anxiety and depression. Still
lagging far behind is readily available information for
the support people.

The roots of this book go back about 20 years when I
was a victim of panic attacks and agoraphobia. I over-
came the illness and, a few years later, became a support
person to a very dear friend. I attended panic attack/ago-
raphobia group meetings with her but found that we support people were ignored and seated at the back. We
were not invited to take part in the meetings. The support people were being treated as nothing more than res-
ident taxi drivers, and at no time did anyone suggest they
could have a role to play. At the same time there was no
suggestion or encouragement for us to get together to
discuss the illnesses and the help we could offer to the
anxious people, or how to look after ourselves.

The confusion, lack of understanding and hopelessness on the other support people's faces convinced me
that an important part of the healing process was being
overlooked.

After finding no information for caregivers in print, I turned to the Internet to see what was posted on it regarding anxiety caregiving. I could find nothing. Convinced that this information was important to the healing process, in 1995 I set up a small Internet site inviting caregivers to share information. Within a few weeks caregivers, those who had the disorders, and professionals were visiting the site looking for information. This mix of people proved to be an excellent composition for exchanging information of the type we needed. Using all of the various facilities available on the Internet we set up mail lists, CHAT groups and bulletin boards to facilitate the exchange.

The response and endorsement of the site was stunning. It has won many mental health awards and now has almost 400 links to it, most from professional organizations.

In 1996 I was asked if I could put some of the information we had gathered into print to make it more widely available. The first edition sold out within the year. A second edition was produced in 1997 and has been reprinted several times. The need for the information had certainly been demonstrated. Professional and editorial reviews were very kind. We received several hundred letters thanking us for the book and containing such comments as," Finally I understand what my husband has been going through." "This book saved my marriage." "This is the first time I have really been able to understand the information, relate to it and use it."

The clarity and practicality of the information no doubt comes from the material being written in nontechnical language and the fact that all examples, letters and conversation are real. Also, no material has been included until it has been "consumer tested" and we have received the OK that it accurately reflects the way people feel, and the explanations are clear and the suggestions workable.

The material for this third edition is presented using the same procedure that proved to be so successful with the first two.

With seven years behind us our information base has grown to the point that we probably have the largest database of this type of information available.

I hope you find this book useful and that you will give me feedback so we can all (sufferers of anxiety illnesses and support people) work together to increase the resources available to the support person.

Ken Strong
Victoria, BC, Canada
January 2003

The Legal Bit

DISCLAIMER: This book is for informational purposes only. It is in no way intended to replace professional advice.

Neither the author nor the publisher have, nor make any pretense to having, any professional standing in either the field of medicine or psychology. At all times a professional should be consulted for advice.

Similarly, the information on medication has been obtained from various sites on the Internet and is presented for informational purposes only.

The author, publisher and copyright holder therefore assume no responsibility or liability for the information contained in this book.

Don't Skip this Section

A NUMBER OF SECTIONS of the work of our support people's group are used in seminars, lectures and support meetings. It has become evident that it is possible for people to leave the meetings with a mistaken picture of those with anxiety disorders. Just as any book will list most of the symptoms of any disease or disorder, the same is done here. That does not mean an anxious person will show all the symptoms or will have the same level of anxiety from day to day or even hour to hour. It is very important to understand this.

For instance, the chapter on Generalized Anxiety Disorder lists a large number of possible behavior characteristics. No person is going to show all of them. Even those types of behavior which are evident will not be present all the time and will wax and wane with the degree of anxiety the people are experiencing. The people may not even show or have any external symptoms at all. They can perform their work and continue with a social life while few of those around them are aware of the chemical imbalance from which they suffer and which can cause the anxiety disorders.

So why is this? Most lay people are not familiar with anxiety disorders and tend to overreact to them. Secondly, because they were considered by many to be a "mental problem" (whatever that is) rather than a chemical imbalance, there is still a certain amount of unfounded stigma concerning these disorders.

To try to rectify this, let's use diabetes as an analogy. Diabetes is well known, fairly common, not apparent to those around the people who have it, chemically based and yet carries no stigma. It is readily accepted that there are certain degrees of diabetes, and that it can vary in degree and is treatable. No one expects a person with diabetes to automatically have all the symptoms, including the more extreme ones such as blindness, kidney disease and loss of limbs. It is accepted that the person may have ups and downs until the diabetes is brought under control. It is also accepted that it can generally be controlled through lifestyle modification and medication.

So, please, when reading such chapters as those on generalized anxiety disorder, do not automatically expect the anxious person to be always unable to function, to be snappy and to think negatively. It doesn't work like that.

Following this advice will give you a much more realistic understanding of the anxiety disorders, and those with the disorders will be very appreciative and have one less thing to worry about.

The flip side is the number of people with anxiety who become upset when they read this information, particularly the section I have included on "blaming." I understand that not everyone is into blaming, but I do want to bring this issue to the attention of support people in the hope that it will enable them not to take it personally or be too upset by it. As my grandmother used to say when a sick person snapped at me, "It is just the illness talking."

One

Stress and Anxiety

STRESS, FEAR AND ANXIETY all play important roles in the normal functioning of the body, but in anxiety disorders the brain gets mixed up and overreacts. Partly due to this mix-up, anxiety disorders are said to be fear based. Treatment is directed towards helping the brain sort itself out. That's it, in a nutshell. The remainder of this book goes into these points in more detail and helps support people to understand the disorders as well as offering suggestions on how to act for the benefit of all.

The mechanisms in the body, which regulate the amount of stress and the times you feel it, play a large role in the anxiety illnesses. To understand the anxiety illnesses you have to comprehend the origin and control of the stress mechanisms in the body. A knowledge of stress will also help the support person to monitor and control her own level of stress.

"Stress" is a much over used and misunderstood word. Biologically, "stress" is anything that causes the body to use more energy. It may be as simple as a carbon dioxide build-up in the blood causing you to expend a bit more energy to breathe a bit faster. The "stress" is the high carbon dioxide level; the response requiring more energy is an increase in breathing. No big deal. Another example is the extra energy required when you get up in the morning. The muscles need more blood so the heart pumps faster. Nothing fancy about that, so how does the body know how much energy it should be releasing? That's the result of two ner-

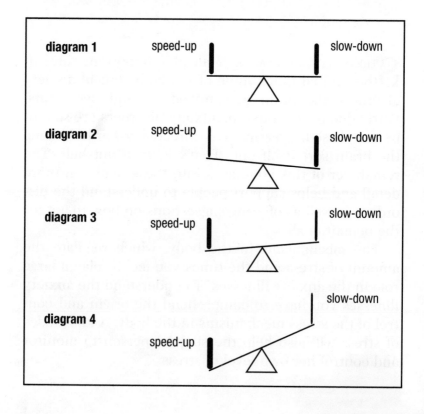

vous system divisions in the body that tend to act opposite to each other to keep the body in balance.

The body is constantly doing a balancing act. Drink too much water and the kidneys work overtime. Sweat profusely and little urine is produced. The kidneys are trying to keep the amount of water in the bloodstream constant. The same is true of most systems in the body as they adjust your breathing, pulse rate, blood sugar level, etc. to meet the current demands placed on it. Sometimes you do things that upset the balance. Drink too much coffee on a shopping trip and the caffeine causes the kidneys to release so much water you quickly learn the location of every washroom in the area.

Two major nervous system divisions in the body adjust your stress level according to your needs. Each system works oppositely to the other. The *parasympathetic* system keeps you relaxed; it is always saying, "All is well. Stay cool. Have a nap." The *sympathetic* system keeps your level of stress up. It is always saying, "Battle Stations. Head for the hills; the dam's busted." To keep things simple we will call the sympathetic system the "speed-up" system and the parasympathetic will be the "slow-down" system. A key player in the "speed-up" system is a hormone you probably know— adrenaline.

If only one of the systems had its say you would either be utterly relaxed or completely hysterical. The two have to work together so you can make the constant adjustments, which are necessary just to get you through the ups and downs of the day.

The diagrams of the see-saw (page 2) show the activity of the two at various levels of stress. The first diagram shows a normal situation. You may be walking along a quiet street. In the second diagram you may be just about asleep. The third shows a person in a slightly tense or anxious situation such as crossing a busy street with no crosswalk. In the fourth case something drastic has happened—a car accident, being robbed, having a bad scare or being chased by a large angry goose.

Let's have a closer look at these two branches of the nervous system. Each release chemicals that cause the body to change in response to its current needs.

The speed-up system readies the body to face a challenge. It is a survival mechanism. When we are threatened, many chemicals are released which prepare the body in a multitude of ways. The senses become sharper; sugar is released into the blood stream for the muscles to use; blood is diverted from the stomach to the muscles to fight or run; breathing increases to bring more oxygen to the muscles; the heart beat increases to move blood faster; pain may not be noticed; blood clotting time decreases.

The slow-down system acts in an opposite manner as it attempts to return the body to a relaxed state. Breathing and heart beat slow as the body relaxes.

It is perfectly normal for us to go through many relaxation/ stress changes in a day as our bodies react to events going on around us. Unless the changes are extreme we are rarely aware of them.

Good Stress and Bad Stress

Stress is the body's natural chemical response to changes around it. It is a built-in survival mechanism.

During a crisis, the brain releases a barrage of chemical messengers that prepares the body to meet the danger by directing extra energy to the heart, muscles, lungs, etc. This burst of energy provides the body with both extra energy and speed to either strike out at the danger or run from it. This extra energy also allows you to achieve a goal or to accomplish a task. There is even recent evidence that these speed-up chemicals can keep the immune system operating at a higher level. (That's why, some researchers suggest, you can carry on during work but become sick on holidays as you relax and the disease can now take hold.)

This natural speed-up reaction is useful if you have an outlet for the energy. Fighting or running during a battle is an outlet, as is preparing for an athletic event or a business meeting. If the extra flow comes from happiness or excitement it is acceptable to jump for joy. But if the stress comes from someone making you feel uptight or embarrassed, modern civilization frowns on you bopping that person on the nose.

Here we are in a bind. The body is responding normally by releasing the "speed-up" chemicals but our code of living prevents us from doing what we were designed to do. We can't use up the extra energy by running from the scene or by striking out. What happens to this energy? That's the dilemma. Unless it can somehow be released it can, over time, cause both physical and emotional problems.

Living in a stressful state for a long period can cause illnesses which may not surface until years later, such as ulcers, high blood pressure, anxiety disorders, etc.

Don't jump to the conclusion that this is the basis of anxiety illnesses. The following chapters will show it is not as simple as that.

To illustrate how the stress levels of the body have played a role throughout evolutionary history, I have included a 'fairy tale' type story. Writing fairy tales is definitely not one of my strong points but I have used this story in various presentations and people say they have found it useful.

A Tale of Marmots, Anxiety and Such

Do you know what a marmot is? A marmot is an animal very much like a gopher. For our story we could choose a gopher, a mouse, an elephant or even a camel. It doesn't matter—they all respond the same. I chose a marmot because I like them.

On a sunny afternoon Martin the marmot was out for a stroll when the shadow of an eagle passed overhead. Martin didn't have to stop to think that an eagle looking for a meal was bad news because through years of evolution Martin's brain was preprogrammed to respond immediately to the threat. Martin didn't give any conscious thought to what was going on around him—his body automatically prepared Martin for the danger and he was out of there at top speed to find a safe place. As long as that eagle was out there, there was no way that Martin would feel comfortable coming out of his hole.

If Martin could have looked inside himself he would have noticed adrenaline was being released; more blood was being diverted to the muscles; respiration rate increased; heart rate increased; the pupils of the eyes had opened wide to let more light in and to give him more acute vision, etc.

Martin knew he was all hyped up and he knew the reason why. That was enough for him. He was just staying put until the danger passed. When the danger was gone his body would again return to a more relaxed mode and Martin could get on with his sunny afternoon stroll. The automatic reaction had saved Martin. That was its purpose—to prepare him to run or fight so he could live to run or fight another day. And a very useful purpose it is too.

A very long distance away in a place completely unknown to Martin was a woman called Terri. Terri didn't know anything about Martin either. But that didn't matter; even though Terri knew nothing of Martin she had a great deal in common with him. She had a heart, lungs, legs and a mouth—just to name a few things. In fact well over 75% of Terri's genes were the same as those that made Martin into what he was. They had much in common and, yes, she even had almost identical genes to those in Martin that made him act as he did when the eagle flew over his head.

Terri was just getting out of her car when a big barking dog started running toward her. The dog didn't look friendly and those very same genes that were in Martin took over in Terri. Her heart started to beat faster, she began to breathe more rapidly and the blood was rerouted so that most of it went to her muscles so she could run or fight. Terri bolted back into her safe place—her car and slammed the door shut. Soon the owner came and took the dog away. Teri was too preoccupied to notice the changes which were going on inside but they were same as exactly the same as the ones which had gone on in Martin and served exactly the same protective purpose...to prepare the body to fight or run.

The thinking part of Terri's brain now took over and as she realized the danger was past her body started returning to normal. With the dog safely gone, Terri could now get out of her car with no problems. The danger was past and she felt quite safe.

While Martin and his friends illustrated the mechanisms in the body that respond to stress, keep in mind that the way in which the responses showed themselves here are more akin to those of high anxiety and panic attacks. In the other forms of anxiety there are similar mechanisms at work but they don't necessarily show themselves to the same extent.

At this point you may be asking something like, "If anxiety causes stress/worry, and stress/worry cause anxiety, doesn't it feed on itself?" Yes, it does. Such a situation is called a positive feedback loop and positive feedback loops are generally bad news for the body. Treatment is aimed at breaking the cycle through a number of means. Methods of treatment are discussed in Chapter 8.

In the next chapter we will look at the various types of anxiety disorders.

Main Points

• Anxiety disorders are fear based.
• The body is reacting as though there were some emergency.
• People with the disorders usually know their reactions are not called for.
• It is harmful to say things like "It is all in your head."
• Those with anxiety disorders are sane but fear they may not be.
• People do get over anxiety disorders.

Two

The Many Forms of Anxiety

ABOUT 25% OF THE POPULATION will develop an anxiety disorder at some time in their lives. Even in the most advanced countries only about a quarter of them seek help.

In Chapter One you saw that a certain amount of stress is necessary as the body "revs" up to meet the current needs.

Anxiety disorders occur when the body revs up for no rational reason. Over time this heightened anxiety state can lead to long-term problems that affect the body both physically and mentally. Most of these problems were, until a few years ago, poorly recognized. This lack of understanding led to frequent mis-diagnoses such as, "It's just nerves, PMS," etc. Also left confused and dejected were those who were told there was nothing wrong with them and they should stop wasting everyone's time.

The uninformed may still think there is nothing wrong with an anxiety sufferer that can't be corrected by telling the victim how silly it all is. This belief is a major misunderstanding. No matter how bizarre the behavior and thoughts may seem to us, they are real to the person with the disorder. Making them feel even worse is the knowledge that what they are feeling, thinking and going through is neither rational nor normal. In the long run, some type of fear appears to be common to all of the illnesses described below.

A word of caution before we proceed. As you read through the symptoms of phobias you will probably find one or two items that you feel describe you. Just remember that before you say, "Hey, that's me!" just one or two of the symptoms probably means you are a normal human being. To be classified as having the disorder there are few diagnostic hoops to jump through including having your way of life severely restricted through anxiety.

Classification of Anxiety Illnesses

Using strict diagnostic criteria, experts classify each of the illnesses individually but, in reality, there is much overlap of symptoms among the types of anxiety disorders. One problem common to them all may be a certain degree of depression. The depression may arise from the person's restricted life style or it may be associated in some other way.

The possible causes of anxiety illnesses are discussed elsewhere in this book. Briefly they may be genetic, a biochemical imbalance in the brain, stressful events which have occurred in life or all of the above. To avoid repetition in each of the sections on phobias I have just included the current thinking as to possible psychological factors. Remember that any or all of the above causes may be at the root of the problem.

Phobias

"Phobia" comes from the Greek "in dread of." Today it has come to mean an irrational fear or aversion. Regardless of how irrational it is, the fear is very real to a person suffering from it.

Phobias are divided into four basic types.

1. **Simple or Specific Phobias**

   About 10% of the population have some level of this type of phobia.

   In a simple or specific phobia there is an irrational fear of one particular situation or object. Fear of spiders, heights, elevators and blood are examples. The phobia may or may not be too restricting. A fear of tigers will not be too restricting if there are none in the area, but a fear of the number "13" can be very restrictive depending upon how far the person takes it. I have known those who would not put a book down if they were on page 13 or even a multiple of it.

   Digital clocks have opened up a whole new arena for the fear of "13" as the phobic person may add the numbers together to see that the total is not "13" prior to making an important phone call, etc.

   By the way, the fear of the number 13 is known as triskaidekaphobia.

2. **Social Phobia**

   Estimates for the number of people with social phobia vary between 5 to 7% of the population.

Social phobia frequently begins in childhood or adolescence. People with social phobia tend to think others are very competent in various social situations but they are not. They believe people are constantly judging and evaluating their performance and find them lacking. They are afraid of embarrassing themselves in front of others. The anxiety present is due to this belief.

The events, which cause anxiety, can be rather specific. They feel quite comfortable doing some things but are very anxious about doing others. For instance, they may have difficulty walking down a street because they might imagine others are looking at them and criticizing the way they walk, they way they are dressed, etc. Another person may have no trouble walking down the street but, for similar concerns, have difficulty eating in public. Of course, they may not be limited to just one uncomfortable situation and each person will have his/her set of events with cause anxiety.

Examples of some of these situations are:
- fear of using public washrooms
- fear of eating in public
- fear of speaking in public
- fear of answering the door
- fear of meeting people who are not immediate family members
- fear of being drawn into a conversation with anyone
- fear of making eye contact during conversations
- and many others

Like other forms of phobias, the sufferers from social phobia realize their concerns are irrational but, without help, it usually means little in the way they react to their triggers.

These people tend to appear very shy but there are differences between shyness and social phobia. A shy person will usually not avoid social situations that make them uneasy while those with social phobia frequently do avoid such situations to the extent even of choosing a career path that "protects" them from facing uncomfortable settings. Also, if a person with this disorder becomes so uncomfortable they verge on a panic attack, they do not seek medical attention since they know the cause. Likewise, a person who suffers from general high anxiety, will see their anxiety level rise and fall but the person with social phobia will possibly always have the phobia, unless treated for it.

Treatment may involve medications for calming as well as therapy including being slowly exposed to the situations which they find uncomfortable. Where possible, it has been found to be very helpful if they can ask the people what they think of them and if their fears are based on fact. Most times they find they were noticed no more than any other person in a particular setting.

3. **Agoraphobia**

It is estimated about 1% of the population has agoraphobia.

Agoraphobia is the fear of being away from home or a safe place or a safe person. In many people's minds agoraphobia is linked with the fear of having a panic attack. People with panic attacks can develop agoraphobia but it can also occur on its own or in conjunction with other illnesses. In the ultimate form these are the people one hears of who have not left their home or a certain room for months or years. You will find agoraphobia addressed in detail in various sections of this book.

4. **Separation Anxiety Disorder of Childhood**

It is normal for young children to become anxious if they are separated from their parents. In separation anxiety this is carried to such an extreme that a child may refuse to go to sleep unless a parent is present in the room; or there is a persistent reluctance to leave the parents to go to school. The child may also show anxiety, exhibit tantrums or become socially withdrawn in anticipation of, during, or immediately following separation from a parent or other person to whom she is attached. Medication and counselling are the treatments of choice.

Obsessive Compulsive Disorder

Obsessive-compulsive disorder (OCD) is another member of the anxiety group. People with OCD are subjected to unwanted recurring thoughts, images or impulses that are almost always of a type that produce feelings of anxiety or fear. "Some bad thing is going to happen if I don't do this." Sometimes they may know what they believe is going to happen (my wife will be in a car accident), an undefined bad event or a feeling of unease.

To reduce the anxiety these people develop actions or rituals that they must perform in order to counteract the fears from actually occurring. To add to the anxiety they almost always know both the thoughts and their responding behavior are not rational. As with the other anxiety disorders, it can, if untreated, take over their whole day and has the potential to make some drastic unhealthy changes to the life of the family. OCD is covered in more detail in Chapter 7.

Generalized Anxiety Disorder

Generalized Anxiety Disorder (GAD) affects about 4% of the population and is the most common form of anxiety seen at anxiety clinics.

To misquote the rabbit from *Alice in Wonderland,* "Oh dear! Oh, dear! I'm late, I'm late for a very important date." We all have tense moments, anxious days or even longer. It is perfectly normal. We may be fidgety, have a fast heartbeat, begin to sweat, hyperventilate, etc. Eventually the event, which causes the anxiety, passes and the body returns to normal from its state of heightened readiness.

People who develop GAD have much more than a normal state of anxiety. The following description of generalized anxiety is taken from the internet site of the National Institute of Mental Health, MD, USA, and used with permission.

Generalized Anxiety Disorder

"I always thought I was just a worrier. I'd feel keyed up and unable to relax. At times it would come and go, and at times it would be constant. It could go on for days. I'd worry about what I was going to fix for a dinner party, or what would be a great present for somebody. I just couldn't let something go."

"I'd have terrible sleeping problems. There were times I'd wake up wired in the morning or in the middle of the night. I had trouble concentrating, even reading the newspaper or a novel. Sometimes I'd feel a little lightheaded. My heart would race or pound. And that would make me worry more."

Generalized anxiety disorder (GAD) is much more than the normal anxiety people experience day to day. It's chronic and exaggerated worry and tension, even though nothing seems to provoke it. Having this disorder means always anticipating disaster, often worrying excessively about health, money, family, or work. Sometimes, though, the source of the worry is hard to pinpoint. Simply the thought of getting through the day provokes anxiety.

People with GAD can't seem to shake their concerns, even though they usually realize that their anxiety is more intense than the situation warrants. People with GAD also seem unable to relax. They often have trouble falling or staying asleep. Their worries are accompanied by physical symptoms, especially trembling, twitching, muscle tension, headaches, irritability, sweating, or hot flashes. They may feel lightheaded or out of breath. They may feel nauseated or have to go to the bathroom frequently. Or they might feel as though they have a lump in the throat.

Many individuals with GAD startle more easily than other people. They tend to feel tired, have trouble concentrating, and sometimes suffer depression, too.

Usually the impairment associated with GAD is mild and people with the disorder don't feel too restricted in social settings or on the job. Unlike many other anxiety disorders, people with GAD don't characteristically avoid certain situations as a result of their disorder. However, if severe, GAD can be very debilitating, making it difficult to carry out even the most ordinary daily activities.

GAD comes on gradually and most often hits people in childhood or adolescence, but can begin in adulthood, too. It's more common in women than in men and often occurs in relatives of affected persons. It's diagnosed when someone spends at least 6 months worried excessively about a number of everyday problems...

GAD is characterized by a continuing anxiety that persists for months. In the strictest sense it is, by definition, not accompanied by phobias, obsessions or panic attacks. The person is just uptight but can't put her finger on why she is continually anxious.

As in severe cases of depression, the memory may become temporarily impaired. Specific information may not be able to be retrieved (such as person's name) or the information may never have made it into the memory in the first place (in one ear and out the other). Criticisms of, "You don't listen." and "Are you becoming senile?" are neither warranted not helpful. It is frustrating to these people to know they have a memory lapse or are certain they were never given the information. The anxiety involved only makes it worse. Some people, however, do find they can help alleviate the anxiety of memory problems by joking about themselves and it does seem to help that they are willing to do so.

While GAD is an anxiety disorder unto itself, it is frequently also found with other anxiety disorders and the boundaries become blurred.

Generalized anxiety disorder is discussed in more detail in Chapter 5.

Post-Traumatic Stress Disorder

Many will know this by the name "shell shock" when it was commonly associated with returning veterans. Anyone who has undergone a severe trauma, which produces terror, fear or feelings of helplessness, can develop signs of PTSD. Even living next to a noisy construction site for a period of time has been known to cause stress and PTSD, as the person has no control over the noise.

Post-traumatic stress disorder causes a number of symptoms including avoidance of objects or situations which remind the person of the cause, recurrent nightmares and an emotional numbness. The symptoms may not occur until some time after the event. In the case of children the symptoms may not surface until adulthood. PTSD is covered in detail in its own chapter.

Panic Attacks

Panic attacks come out of the blue with virtually no warning. The symptoms of an attack may include:
- trembling
- heart racing and thumping
- weak knees
- tingling in the hands, arms, mouth
- a feeling of dissociation; here but not here
- a need to run and escape. But to where?
- a feeling of being trapped
- utter terror
- the walls or floor seem to be moving
- the walls are closing in
- feeling off balance
- knowing "something" is not right
- a choking feeling, whether eating or not

Not everyone has all these symptoms and some have additional symptoms during an attack, which can last from a few minutes to several hours or longer. It finally ebbs away and the sufferer is left with a feeling of mental and physical exhaustion, trembling, relief and a horrendous fear it will return.

Looking at the symptoms it is easy to see why attacks are frequently first diagnosed in the emergency room of a hospital.

Below is a table of anxiety/panic symptoms and the reasons behind them.

Why Do They Feel This Way?

Symptoms	Causes
Heart pounding	Heart speeding up to move blood and oxygen faster.
Breathing faster	Obtaining more oxygen for the muscles.
Chest pain	Muscles tightening.
Rubbery legs	Blood supply building up in the legs/decreased oxygen to the brain.
Feeling of dissociation	Less blood going to the brain and/or some think a trance state is almost reached.
Bright lights are disturbing	Pupils have opened for more acute vision.
Walls are bending inwards	An effect of the pupils opening wide.
Sweating	The body is harder to hold onto in a fight. It is slippery.
Numbness in hands	Due to the diversion of blood to the muscles.
Tingling in mouth	A result of hyperventilating.
Choking sensation	Due to muscle tension.
Shaking	Due to muscle tension
Bowel and bladder problems	The nerve controlling these functions is highly stimulated during stress.

As you will see in the text, the anxiety and panic attack symptoms are really just exaggerated normal responses of the body reacting to a threat.

Three

Anxiety and Panic Attacks

BEFORE MOVING INTO THIS CHAPTER let's see if we can give you some concept of what it is like to have GAD, panic attacks and agoraphobia.

Imagine a person who finds himself on a rickety footbridge over a high gorge. The floorboards are rotten and the ropes holding it aren't in good shape either. Over time Kelly learns she can just manage to keep going on if she focuses on taking one slow careful step at a time. She is sweating, has a racing heart and showing other signs of reacting to danger. Add to this someone on safe ground who keeps prattling away with things like, "Where is the milk?" "Ran into Ron today, he says blah...blah." "Did you know the hot water tank is leaking?" "Hey, Frankenstein is on TV tonight. Want to watch it with me?"

A floorboard snaps leaving Kelly supported only by the rotten ropes. Gusts of wind flip the bridge from side to side. The rope fibers make small popping sounds as they break. Kelly's anxiety level soars up to the point of panic. Her mind has one desire, "Where is safety? How do I get there." "Run, Kelly, run!" And a barely registering voice demands, "Where are the potato chips I asked you to pick up?"

Let's get Kelly off the bridge and move her to safe ground where she lives.

Somehow she made it from the bridge back to the same ground on which she lives. Unfortunately the only way for Kelly to leave her safe ground and go anywhere is over rickety bridges. Some bridges are in somewhat better shape than others. After several horrific experiences of being trapped on the rickety bridges would Kelly keep trying to cross them or just stay in her safe place?

Of course it is not possible to say this is exactly like the feelings of a person who lives with high anxiety. The bridge is the journey through the day of a person with high snxiety. The overwhelming experiences are the panic attacks while the breaking boards and the wind are the normal day to day events that require a bit more energy to deal with them. The fear of leaving a safe place and having another panic attack is the agoraphobia.

With this analogy of the rickety bridges in mind we will move on with the chapter.

For diagnostic reasons, the professional uses specific criteria to distinguish between general anxiety, anticipatory anxiety, and panic attacks. To the nonprofessional the lines between them are somewhat blurred since each one contains elements of the others. They vary in intensity, speed of onset, physical and behavioral manifestations. A further complication is how the person acts in response to the level of anxiety present. We can't get in their heads to see how strong it is, and one person may be incapacitated at a certain level of anxiety while another person, with a similar level, just carries on. Also, a person, during an anxious period, is not always at the same level of anxiety and one onset may vary in intensity from the next.

As a layman writing for laymen readers, I will distinguish between them in a simple way.

Anxiety is a general feeling of unease; it may be slight or very strong.

Anticipatory Anxiety is the rise in the anxiety level as a person contemplates a fearful situation she is about to enter. Most people have experienced a very miniform of it when they have an attack of nerves prior to making their first speech or appearance on stage. For most it is handled with nothing worse than rubbery knees and a slight quavering of the voice. For those prone to anxiety dosprders it may rise to the point where they are incapacitated by the attack.

Agoraphobia is sometimes referred to as the fear of having another panic attack and so people remain in 'safe places.' When I developed agoraphobia, though, I did not relate it to a fear of panic attacks. To me it was just like trying to force my way through jelly to get off my property. At times it seemed like a force was pushing me backwards towards the house and the nearer I got to the property line the stronger it became. (Well, maybe I operate on a more primitive level than others do, or else my brain just didn't bother to befuddle me with the details.)

Attacks are a sudden increase in the level of anxiety. While high anxiety can be very debilitating and should not be downplayed, the granddaddy of anxiety disorders is the panic attack.

Panic attacks vary in severity and from person to person. Some people can continue on the job with them; others are virtually immobilized—unable to leave a small area or areas, which are their safe places. Even those who can continue to function tend to do so by structuring their lives around the possibility of another attack. Any triggers which bring on an attack are avoided if at all possible. About 8% of the population will have panic attacks at one time or another. Over half of these will develop some degree of depression. About 25 to 30% of those with panic attacks admit they have considered suicide as an option.

The triggers vary but generally include wide-open spaces and closed in places such as parkades, grocery store aisles, escalators, etc. Any place where one is "trapped" can bring on an attack: elevators, escalators, theaters, busses, the inside traffic lane, stop lights, left turns, dentists, hairdressers, the bank machine when it has your card, writing exams, being on the phone, giving a speech or presentation, etc.

Once an attack occurs in a certain place the person seems to become sensitized and it or similar places can bring on another attack. These places are then avoided

due to the fear of an attack. The fear caused by thinking of an event which could bring on another attack is
called "anticipatory anxiety." If this fear restricts a person almost to the point of not leaving the property,
house or even a certain room in the house, agoraphobia is present. She is comfortable only in her safe places
and/or with the people she trusts to help her—her support people.

Allowing for many exceptions it is possible to give
a very general profile of a person prone to panic
attacks. They are usually intelligent, caring, people
pleasers, creative and very imaginative. Being imaginative, while very useful for creative work, can backfire. Tell such a person that a ringing in the ears is a
symptom and they will probably develop ear ringing.
The same is true of reactions to medications. This creative thinking can be behind their "what if" pattern of
thinking. If a wind gets up the "what if's" can flow in
this type of pattern: what if a branch comes off the
tree? What if the branch hits the house? What if
someone is hurt? What if the whole tree comes down?
What if it lands on someone's car? What if someone is
killed? Oh, no! I'm going to be sued! This type of
thinking can quickly go from something simple like a
breeze to a catastrophic event.

As a support person it is extremely important to
remember that all of the fears, feelings and "what if's"
are real to the person. It would be counterproductive
to say, "It's all in your head." They know it is all going
on inside them and that it is not normal to react as
they do. This knowledge, the fear of embarrassing
themselves in front of those who do not understand,
their crippling lifestyles and the effect this has on

their family can lead to shame, low self-image, guilt,[1] frustration and depression. The depression is increased as they begin to lose social contacts, become restricted in what they can do, and perhaps develop a fear of not being able to tell many people about the disorder.

---

[1] The feeling of guilt can stem from many causes including:
- the load being put on others.
- lost wages.

Four

The Cause(s) of Panic Attacks

WANT TO START a tumultuous conversation? In a group of anxiety sufferers tell them you know the cause of panic attacks. I guarantee the reaction will be vociferous. There are many theories of the causes and staunch advocates of each.

The reasoning behind each possible cause can be somewhat complex so let's see if we can keep it simple and concise.

You know the body responds to a *perceived* threat by revving up the "speed-up" system, which includes the release of adrenaline. The body must *perceive* the event to be a threat. So, a young child meeting a tiger may think it is a large pussycat and respond by trying to pet it. A woman stepping out of a car and seeing two large dogs bounding towards her may step right back in again unless she knows the dogs are friendly.

Why does an anxious person go into a panic attack state when there is no discernible trigger? This is really a two-part question. The first part involves the reason for the person developing panic attacks in the first place. The second part looks at some possible triggers once the anxiety response has been established.

Part I Initial Causes

The suggested initial causes include the following.

1. Heredity. Either the anxiety illness itself is passed on or, at the very least, the predisposition for it is in the genes. This *could* explain why several members of a family have anxiety illnesses.

2. An unhealthy atmosphere in the family home during childhood may be behind anxiety illnesses. These range from being afraid of being left alone or abandoned to a constantly stressful family environment. An alcoholic or abusive parent frequently figures in the lives of those with anxiety problems.

3. Very long periods of stress can cause anxiety. These may be associated with job stress, a poor marriage, war service, an unrealistic parental pressure to excel in school, etc.

4. Medical problems may be at the root of or mimic some anxiety disorders. These problems may be inherited or can be the result of encounters in life. Included here are some heart problems, some mineral deficiencies, illnesses of the thyroid, parathyroid or adrenal glands, extreme PMS, hormonal changes, and certain other diseases. Such problems should be ruled out by a physician.

It should be noted here that many people still attach a stigma to "mental problems." As such it is not unusual for a person with an anxiety illness to try to find a "more socially acceptable" cause.

5. The biopsychosocial model of anxiety disorders states that, while a chemical imbalance may be a contributing factor in some anxiety cases, there are other interacting elements which must be considered such as genetics, certain stressful situations or thoughts, medical problems which can aggravate anxiety, etc. Advocates of this model claim that if the sole cause behind anxiety were a chemical imbalance, then all anxiety disorders should be relieved through medications. They go on to point out that counselling aimed at changes in thought patterns and reactions would not be as effective as it is where medication has failed. In other words, medication is not the answer in many cases and therapy will usually help where medication has failed.

Part II Maintaining Factors

Once a person has been "sensitized" to anxiety it is fairly easy for certain things to trigger an increase in anxiety level. These triggers are numerous and include having to repress feelings, negative self-talk, remembering stressful or unhappy events, a slight choking feeling from swallowing food or pills, heights, a feeling of being trapped in an elevator or bank line up, etc. The panic attack itself may occur even from the fear of an attack or without the person realizing what the trigger is—if any.

Now, what is the cause of a panic attack? If you think I gave you an answer above I have not made it clear. Medicine continues to look for the cause or causes and is pursuing some very promising lines of inquiry, but for now it could be any or all of the above, some of the above or none of the above.

There is one other way frequently used to "explain" panic attacks.

The chemistry of the brain is very complicated and it does not operate in isolation from the rest of the body. Recent research would tend to indicate that increased anxiety can cause the brain to react even more to anxiety than it did earlier. This involves a series of chemical reactions.

One part of the brain is known as the "alarm room." It notifies us when there is danger. This is a perfectly normal reaction. However, to prevent us from reacting to everything with alarm, another part of the " analysis center" relies on previous experiences to weigh each possible danger. Long-term chemical reactions due to stress seem to cause the analysis center to be less functional. With little counter information, the alarm room sends out its signal. The good news is that medication and/or a change in thinking patterns, helps the analysis center to return to normal.

Five

Generalized Anxiety Disorder

CHAPTER TWO HAD a brief discussion of GAD. Rather than start this chapter off with a repetition of the symptoms, I thought it might be a good idea to put you in a position where you might imagine that you exhibit some of the symptoms of high anxiety. In the situation below there is a good reason for the woman to be anxious. However, remember that people who have generalized anxiety disorder feel highly anxious most of the time. Some of the symptoms are experienced only in severe cases. Of course not everyone has all of the symptoms all of the time. And, yes, some of the symptoms are more closely related to depression than anxiety but we will catch up with them in Chapter 11.

You live in Victoria, B.C. Your name is Gloria. You are a divorced mother of a three-year-old girl whom you have just left in the hands of a new baby sitter. You are on your way to an important business meeting in Vancouver.

The following events occur.

7:00 am Leave house in Victoria for a day business trip to Vancouver.
7:55 am Float plane leaves Victoria's Inner Harbor.
8:30 am Arrive Vancouver Harbor.
8:36 am You are paged by the airline for a message.
8:42 am "Mrs. Turner, your baby sitter phoned. She thinks your daughter must have gotten out of the house because she can't find her."
8:45 am Phone home. No answer.
8:48 am Book return to Victoria on next flight.
8:50 am Phone home. No answer.
8:55 am Leave Vancouver Harbor.
9:30 am Arrive Victoria Inner Harbor.
9:40 am Phone home. No answer.
9:55 am Start the 25-minute drive home.

You are obviously going to be very upset and anxious. What symptoms of this anxiety do you think you would exhibit as you passed through these 3 hours? Check them off below.

❑ trembling
❑ restlessness
❑ generally being uptight
❑ from time to time will snap at people
❑ shortness of breath
❑ can't relax
❑ sweating
❑ difficulty concentrating
❑ heart palpitations
❑ tingling in the hands
❑ sensory hallucinations such as the hands seeming to swell to basketball size

❑ fatigue
❑ feelings of anxiousness without knowing why
❑ nausea
❑ headache
❑ twitching
❑ change of appetite
❑ frequent trips to the bathroom
❑ easily startled
❑ a feeling of a lump in the throat
❑ difficulty swallowing
❑ restlessness
❑ muscle tension
❑ frequent humming or other vocal sounds
❑ automatic negative thinking (ANT)
❑ hypervigilance
❑ the worry about something happening is out of proportion to the likelihood of the event actually occurring
❑ catastrophic thinking
❑ insomnia
❑ other sleep problems
❑ some depression
❑ difficulty making a decision
❑ perfectionism
❑ changes in routine can be unsettling
❑ become controlling
❑ become manipulative
❑ feelings of racing, racing, racing, without a particular cause
❑ procrastination
❑ keep imagining the worst scenarios
❑ problems remembering information

How did you make out? Did you check off a few or were you as cool as a cucumber as you returned to Victoria? Certainly there is cause for Gloria's anxiety. Having some of the symptoms at times like this is perfectly normal.

A person with generalized anxiety disorder may exhibit some or many of the above symptoms. But the problem with GAD is that unlike, in Gloria's temporary situation, there is no "genuine" basis for the amount of anxiety experienced. Also, the person is more or less constantly anxious.

The body of a very anxious person is more or less usually at some fairly high degree of readiness for some unidentified and not present danger. The feeling could be similar to your degree of anxiety as you walk alone down a dark ghetto street at night where there have been several assaults in recent days. You have a reason to be at heightened danger stations. However, the person with GAD may (that's may, not will) feel this way more or less constantly.

NOTE: Professionals may point out that a number of the symptoms I have listed are not directly related to GAD. This is true but, as care-givers, we are looking at the whole picture and the whole person. It is not necessary to be able to classify the symptoms on the basis of diagnosis. Beside, I had to mention these symptoms some-where in the book, so why not here?

GAD does not appear overnight. It has probably been building up for a long period of time. The person knows there is something wrong, but, because it has built up slowly, the individual is sometimes unaware of how fully it has developed.

To be classified as having generalized anxiety disorder you must have had a number of the above symptoms for some time and they must interfere with some aspect of your life, such as work or social life. Of course, not everyone is going to have all of the above traits. Also, those with GAD generally do not try to avoid situations that increase the symptoms; such avoidance is more common in those who experience panic attacks, agoraphobia and social phobia.

In actuality the boundaries between the various anxiety disorders are blurred and symptoms of one or more may be present at the same time. Also, the intensity of the disorder will wax and wane over time as do the symptoms of related disorders as they sneak in and out of the total picture. For instance, OCD may be slightly present at some times and not at all at others.

The Roots of GAD

The roots of GAD may lie in one or more of:
- fear of failure
- fear of not being able to cope with demands
- fear of rejection or abandonment
- fear of death or illness
- a genetic disposition
- patterns of coping (or not coping) as learned in the early family setting
- under stress for a long period of time
- none of the above

General Patterns of New Behavior

As GAD develops you may have noticed some changes in the person's behavior.

One of the most common problems mentioned by support people is that they cannot understand what is going on as the person with anxiety begins to show new behavior. Life seems to be a constant balancing act of walking on eggs and never knowing if what you do will be greeted with thanks or a bark. Mixed messages are common as are changing reactions to the same suggestion, etc., from one time to the next. One day it is OK to say or do one thing but the next day you are taken back by the reaction.

What is Going On?

There are general patterns of behavior that may show themselves in slightly different forms. Also, the degree to which they are present depends upon the individual person and circumstances.

The behavior can loosely be divided into about five general categories.

Personality traits common to many whom develop GAD

1. Behavior caused by the stress of GAD

2. Protective behavior

3. Fear of developing a panic attack in those who have panic attacks

4. Actions designed to keep the stress level down

To fully appreciate the basis of these confusing reactions we will have to take a deeper look at the situation. People with anxiety disorders are generally

• very intelligent
• people pleasers
• peace makers
• compassionate

- very responsible
- perfectionists to some degree (some more than others)

Given the above characteristics it is not difficult to see why the new restrictions placed on them by the anxiety are depressing, frustrating, self-esteem busting and scary, since they are no longer in complete control of how they react to situations.

Couple this constant feeling of anxiety with a fear of increasing the anxiety level or actually feeling oneself going into overload, and it becomes clearer why some of the reactions are very strong.

In other words, the actions could be based on:

- a short temper due to constant anxiety
- constantly being on guard to prevent an increase in anxiety
- a fear of being put in a situation which will increase the anxiety
- a feeling of actually being pushed into overload
- a hair trigger response, since the body is always ready to react
- an almost involuntary release of excess anxiety-based energy which could cause the person to lash out verbally.

To be perfectly honest, the behavior may be an exaggeration of pre-existing personality traits.

Below are a number of actions reported by people on our Internet site. Certainly not all will be present and there are no doubt others that are not mentioned.

Snapping at People From Time to Time
With heightened stress the body is releasing more adrenaline and this extra "energy" must be released

somehow. Snapping or having a short fuse is one way to release it. The person doing the snapping is sometimes very surprised and sorry that he or she did it. The person just reached the boiling point and needed an outlet.

Easily Startled

With the heightened level of alertness comes an increase in the sensitivity of the five senses (hearing, sight, smell, touch, taste). Any unexpected event such as a noise or someone suddenly appearing in the doorway could make a person "jump" because the body is on edge ready to react to any threat.

Frequent Humming or Producing Other Vocal Sounds

This is a stress relieving action. The body tries to find some way to lower the level of stress through a physical act.

Hypervigilance

Due to the heightened level of alertness of the senses, the person is probably the first to notice a new sound or smell. Coupled with the tendency to worry, this can lead to more aggravation as a new sound in the fridge could be interpreted as an indication it is ready to give up the ghost.

Unrealistic Worry

Worry about events occurring which have little likelihood in reality. "When I go out tomorrow morning I may find a flat tire. Maybe the car won't start."

Catastrophic Thinking

Remember the example used on page 21? Here is another example of the worry that can build up. My cat is coughing. Must have some fur in its throat. Aren't there some diseases which cause coughing? Maybe she has one of those. Maybe her shots didn't take. Maybe the shots have expired. She might have one of those terminal diseases. Oh, no. My cat might die. I have to take her to the vet. It is just one major catastrophe after the other with which they have to deal.

Sleeping Problems
It is difficult to sleep when you can't relax and perceived problems keep running through your head.

Automatic Negative Thinking (ANT)
Negative thinking is a major contributor to anxiety. There are several aspects of it but right now I want to focus on the type of negative in which positive happy thoughts are automatically replaced by negative memories from the past—even the far past. See chapter 10 for more detail.

Perfectionism
Many of those with anxiety disorders tend to be perfectionists. Prior to the person's development of the disorder, perfectionism was probably commented on by peers as a positive attribute because the person did excellent work. With the development of the disorder it can backfire. A fear can develop that current work is not up to the previous high standard and the person constantly checks and rechecks. The rechecking and the fear of errors is enough to drive the stress level up even higher.

Difficulty Making Decisions
Prior to the development of anxiety it was quite normal for the person to check several sources before making a purchase. Buying a new sewing machine could be fun. Going around from store to store trying out the various machines, bringing the literature home, talking to

friends and checking Consumer Reports were part of
the excitement of making a new major purchase. Now
the stress, perfectionism and fear of making a mistake
all combine to virtually bring the process to a halt.
What used to be enjoyable is now a stress-producing
event. I have seen some people with 5 or 6 sewing
machines all brought home to try out. Most were from
different stores and all the stores had a generous "no
questions asked" return policy. Frequently all the
machines went back and the process would be repeat-
ed a few months down the road when the person felt up
to looking again.

Changes in Routine Can be Unsettling

The workplace has changed since I first started in it.
Then it was possible to find people who had been con-
tentedly doing the same job for so long it seemed they
predated the last ice age. They were so much in a routine that any changes proved to be upsetting. Even a
change of the colored paper for telephone messages was
hotly debated. At first arguments for maintaining the
initial color could range around "possibilities" such as,
"That color shows up best on my desk." If that failed
the desperation phrase of, "It has always been that way.
That's why." would be heard. To them any change produced stress.

To those who already have an anxiety disorder, a
change of routine can add more stress to their lives.
Frequently they don't say anything, but just live with it
and accept the additional stress.

Changes in Plans Can Upset Them

Many of those with GAD find they need a structured
timetable in which to operate. Last minute changes to

a plan can be very upsetting. Likewise, someone even suggesting an unplanned short stop at a grocery store may be stressful.

They Can Usually Do Only One Thing at a Time

It may take the person a great deal of concentration to be able to do a task. Trying to sidetrack her even briefly can cause the anxiety level to rise. For instance, Nellie is making a business call but her husband needs to know where she put the clean towels. To ask quietly or use hand signals can be very distracting. Try writing a note instead.

The same is true of business conversations. Make sure all people stay on track. If they start bringing in side issues the anxious person may just go into overload and no longer be able to follow the conversation.

There are Times When They Need to Shut Themselves Off from the World for Awhile

A telephone answering machine with the ringer turned off should take care of phone calls. Call display will help to filter calls. Also, where is it written there must be a response to the doorbell? Curling up with a book in a quiet place is also effective for some. Others find going for walks and being alone are helpful. Mindless TV shows are relaxing for some until they become boring.

Being Controlling (Control Freaks)

Part of the problem an anxious person has is feeling she is not in control of her body or her immediate environment. Some are so desperate to maintain control they will go to great lengths to have things done their way. For example, if grocery shopping were normally done on Thursday evenings, there would be all manner of excuses why it could not be done another night. These could range from the possible to the ridiculous. Any excuse was better than explaining the real basis behind the problem.

Hiding the Real Cause

Again, rather than explaining the real cause, these people can go to great lengths to have things done in a manner with which they are comfortable. For instance, if they hear a sound and have a worry the tire may be going flat, they could work on others in the car to convince them they need a restroom break, are hungry, thirsty, anything which requires a stop and the tire can be secretly checked. It is the other people who have initiated the stop, so it hides their needs.

Being Manipulative

Jan sent me this example of how she would manipulate her family so she did not have to admit she could do grocery shopping by herself.

> I would have my adult son take me to the store, under the pretense of buying groceries for him and his brother (which I did) just so I could get the things I needed. It cost me a fortune. I would do almost anything to get my needs met.

(Jan has recovered from her anxiety disorders and now runs a number of Internet lists on anxiety as well as lecturing to medical students on the topic.)

Demanding

In an effort to stay in control, the person may become very demanding. The demands frequently take the form of how things are to be done, or when they are to be done.

They are in Mental Pain

Mental pain is very private pain coming from within. You can be hurt by someone letting you down or insulting you but that does not begin to describe the mental torture these people are going through on the inside due to anguish, despair, frustration, disappointment, fear, and hopelessness. It is something one talks about only to trusted people whom they hope will understand and not rebuff their confidences.

People Close to Them May be Blamed for Various Things

Most of the time it is the result of frustration and letting off the extra energy supplied by the over abundance of adrenaline. Probably they don't treat acquaintances or strangers this way.

They May Resort to Guilt Trips to Get Their Way

Some of these people are extremely adept at finding methods of having people do the things with which they feel comfortable.

Talking to Them is Like Walking on Eggs—They Just Blow Up

Sometimes they have lost so much self-confidence that any comments are taken as criticisms. Also, they may be reacting to a fear of trying something different.

Any Plans or Suggestions You Make are Violently Criticized

Another aspect of the knife-edge under which they live.

Talk About Moving Out

After a length of time when they see little improvement in themselves, they look for other ways to get better. The feeling is that nothing else is working so it must be the environment in which they are living.

Not Wanting to Answer the Door or the Telephone.
There are times when is it almost impossible to take on even a simple thing because it will raise the anxiety level. They just can't deal with one more thing...be it ever so simple.

Reading Subtle Signals
Because they are hypervigilant these people are very good at reading even slight body language signs and voice inflections. Much of the time they interpret them correctly. However, due to their backgrounds, they can be very fast to interpret signals in negative ways when none is intended.

Improvement Is Taking Place But They Don't See It or Believe It
It is so slow to them that they don't see it. Even if they do see it they are sometimes afraid to believe it.

There May Be Difficulties Finding Nonmedical Professionals to Work with People Who Have GAD
Many either don't understand the disorder and/or don't have the patience to work with them when they take forever to make up their minds, forget to ask points or need assurance they have the information straight. Potential financial advisors, for instance, are giving large blocks of free time to answer the same questions over and over, when they could be obtaining new clients or serving the ones they have.

There May be Some Difficulty Finding Trades People to Work with Them
Some people with GAD want so many unrealistic guarantees and ask so many technical questions, the trades people feel any job they do would be unsatisfactory.

Being Asked to Make Snap Decisions May Cause a Freeze up

If the person is put in the position of making snap decisions they may just freeze up and nothing is accomplished. Alternately, incorrect decisions may be made.

During Lengthy Discussions with Financial Advisors, etc. They Just Seem to Fade Out

Many people with anxiety disorders can only take so much. Then they do tend to fade out of energy. At this point they agree to almost anything and/or do not remember much of what occurred.

Natural Peace Makers

Some, but not all, have grown up in a dysfunctional family. It has fallen to these people to attempt to be the peacemakers of the home. As such, they may frequently put their own need second even though it is to their detriment.

They May Agree to Things They Do Not Wish to Do

Should some nonanxious person say, "I know we said we were just going to go to the grocery store and straight home but, it is very important that I go to the mall." The person with GAD is in a bind. Mentally they were not prepared to go to the mall but not wanting to disappoint someone and trying very hard to avoid a stressful situation, they may give in and go. The effects could be detrimental as they become tired, fade out and the stress level rises. Guilt and obligation could also play a role. If they can't drive and must depend upon someone, they could feel beholden to the person and/or afraid that will be the end of the drives.

A Reversion to Child-like Behavior to Get Her Way

"I don't want to!" said in an almost spoiled child or peevish voice.

Inappropriate Behavior to Feel They are in Control

Comments made in a sarcastic manner.

Driven to do Tasks Which Were to be Done by Others

"You didn't do it so I had to." Also a bit of a guilt trip here.

Other Points

I am sure you will find many more types of behavior. Write them down and think about how to handle them...particularly if you are getting up tight as a result. Don't approach this in an obvious, "look what you are doing to me" manner. You are trying to resolve problems not create more.

Main Points

- AAD is the most common of all the anxiety disorders.
- GAD causes a person to be anxious much of the time.
- People with GAD tend to behave in a manner that lessens their stress.
- GAD is treatable by a number of methods.
- One of the best things you can do for the person is to understand.
- If a person with GAD is also prome to panic attacks some of the person's behavior is designed to try to keep the stress level down so she will not flip into a panic attack.
- A person in a state of high anxiety may show physical symptoms such as sweating, etc.

Six

Post-Traumatic Stress Disorder

IN THE FIRST TWO EDITIONS of this book the section on post-traumatic stress disorder was quite short. It was just as short in early drafts of this edition. However, in the light of terrorist activity, I was urged by those with post-traumatic stress disorder and their families to enlarge the section. Once again, the people on the Net got together and came up with a long list of ways in which the support people could be of benefit. All of the suggestions for helping each other are a result of this unselfish effort. The suggestions below are ones which the group found to be useful.

Post-traumatic stress disorder (PTSD) is one of the continuing consequences of being exposed to a psychological traumatic experience. The events may involve death, serious injury, exposure to danger or other horrifying experiences. Up to 28% of those experiencing a traumatizing event develop some degree of PTSD. A macho type has as much chance of developing PTSD as does a sweet, innocent, sheltered person. The symptoms of PTSD usually begin within 3 months of the traumatic event but sometimes it can take several years before they appear. The symptoms can also disappear only to return later.

What Type of Events Can Produce PTSD?

You do not have to have these events happen to you. Just witnessing them is sufficient for some to develop PTSD. Some such events are:

- being in a serious car accident
- seeing a neighbor's dog run over
- a lingering terminal illness in a loved one
- a house fire
- seeing parts of your buddy's body flying in various directions when he steps on a land mine
- sexual abuse as a child
- rape
- a mugging
- a kidnapping
- a near drowning
- being involved in or seeing a catastrophic event
- a sudden realization that there is extreme danger and you are helpless to do anything about it

Why Do People Develop PTSD?

Most of us have experienced some traumatic event in our lives but, although we are upset for a while, we get over them. Occasionally, some people encounter events that are so far off their personal scale of horror or fear that they can't get over them and it has a long term effect on their lives.

Some professionals look at PTSD partially as a shattering realization that our personal world is not so safe. To survive we have to believe that there is not a constant possibility of a traumatic event occurring in our lives. Car accidents happen to other people, as do holdups and rapes.

After recent terrorist events in the world, probably no one needs any additional stories of single events, which could cause PTSD. Not only did the people have to deal with the immediate event, but some were traumatized to the point that whenever a plane went overhead they dove to the ground. Others lived in more or less constant fear of death raining from the sky. Some will get over this but others will go on to develop PTSD and related disorders such as GAD, panic attacks and even agoraphobia.

Sometimes it is not a single event that causes PTSD but a series of ongoing exposures which finally reach the critical limit. Such was the case with Jack.

At the age of 30 Jack was beyond reacting to the rah-rah posters, following the rousing band music to the nearest enlistment depot and believing WWI would be nothing more than a short European holiday—all expenses paid. Whatever his reasons, on Nov. 10, 1915 he signed up for duty overseas and was assigned to the Canadian Signalling Corps.

Since he was a telephone electrician by trade he may have thought he would be installing telephone circuits. He was, but the circuits were the communication wires, which ran between the trenches. (There was no radio in those days.) During battles the wires were constantly being broken and it was his job to crawl over the battlefield and repair them. In the course of his work he was continually crawling through mud as well as bodies and parts of bodies. To add to his problem, during active battles he was never sure which side would be occupying a trench as he approached it to do the repairs. On a couple of occasions even his "home" trench was in enemy hands by the time he returned to it.

At the end of the war Jack returned home to his wife and daughter. But he was a changed man. Throughout most of the rest of his life he could never talk about the war nor look at the medals he had collected. He would yell at his family for no reason and always had to be in control of everything which happened. Nor would he go to bed. Instead, for the next 50 years of his life he would doze in an easy chair, which seemed to help the nightmares stay away. He withdrew into himself and there was virtually no discussion of any kind taking place in his home. The only friends he developed were those at the Canadian Legion who had experienced similar events. Together they would talk about the war and support each other but there was no other help available.

PTSD had not yet been recognized. It was just called "shell shock" or "battle fatigue." It was only about 20 years ago that PTSD was officially recognized as a distinct disorder. Not too many years before that some allied western countries actually shot a few soldiers who were found dazed, wandering around going in the direction from the battle. Guilty of desertion...they said. There is one other war story I want to relate. While I was attending high school in the 1950s I played in a military band largely composed of older retired soldiers. Sitting next to me in the clarinet section was a man who was an excellent player. He was either first or solo clarinet; I don't remember which. What I do remember about him is the blank look he always had on his face, his lack of socialization with others, and the one thing that he would turn to me and say during every break, "I was in the band you know. When we were not playing we were stretcher-bearers. Every time a new group was marched up to the front we would send them off with rousing music. Then we would wait a while until we would go up with the stretchers to bring the poor buggers back." To my knowledge that is all anyone had ever heard him say. Call it "shell shock," "PTSD" or whatever, but he had been that way for as many years as those who knew him could remember.

The Three Major Groups of PTSD Symptoms

The symptoms given below are general. A person may not have them all and may others. The degree to which each plays a role in the person's new "life style" depends upon the person as well as the degree of traumatization.

Intrusive symptoms

This group includes the things that make it seem like the event is occurring all over again. They are the smells, images, memories, nightmares and flashbacks which keep intruding into the mind.

Avoidance

In order to try to prevent triggering any of the reminders, the person avoids situations that may trigger the memories. Unfortunately the person may be so sensitized that many things may trigger them and life becomes almost one of trying to lock themselves behind their own "safe wall."

The person suffering from PTSD will try to avoid thinking or talking about the event. He or she may withdraw from their families emotionally; in fact they become emotionally numb. Other personality changes may also occur such as losing interest in all activities. Alcohol and drugs may enter the picture to help forget and to heighten the numbness.

Arousal

This is very much like persons with GAD living in a constant state of heightened on guard awareness. Having once experienced a traumatic event they are on guard to ensure it does not happen again. The heightened flight or flight response can lead to poor sleep, jumpiness, developing a controlling personality, yelling and becoming angry over little things.

What Type of Treatment Is Used by Professionals?

Medication and counseling are the major tools used in helping a person recover from PTSD. Both cognitive behavioral therapy and group counselling seem to be particularly effective.

The best treatment, though, is one which prevents PTSD from developing. It is very helpful if the person can talk to a counselor immediately after the event. It is not uncommon to hear that counselors are available for those groups who have suffered a trauma such as school shootings. The police forces of many areas also have victim services available to those who have suffered in some way such as an accident a robbery or any event the victim may find traumatizing.

Effects of PTSD on the Family

As with other anxiety disorders, unless the family is aware of what is occurring, it can be a traumatic experience for the family group as well. Even if the family is educated on PTSD, over time it can wear down the family unit and cause dysfunctionality. The support people must learn to take of themselves by such as by following the suggestions in Chapter 14.

What symptoms of PTSD can affect the family?

Once PTSD has been diagnosed the family usually rallies around the person and offers help. But, since PTSD can take quite a long time to heal, the family can become disillusioned and frustrated. It must be kept in mind that support people can only support...they cannot heal. The healing must come from within. Having said that, if the family is prepared for what may happen to them, they will be able to recognize problems that can occur and take the steps necessary to ward them off.

This list is presented in no special order and probably will not apply entirely to each situation. Each one is different.

- The spouse works harder to make up for the lack of work being done by the afflicted person. This may even involve taking a second job.

- Disturbed sleep patterns can cause other family members not to sleep well.
- Frustration occurs at not feeling that the rest of the family is really helping.
- Frustration occurs at not being able to cheer the person up.
- The family becomes upset at the sudden rage which can occur.
- The family over time becomes angry at the extra workload being carried.
- The family finds itself being blamed for problems because the person with PTSD can't accept she is at fault.
- To cope with the blaming and outburst, the family could become emotionally numb.
- Increased drinking and, perhaps, use of drugs has a negative effect on the whole family.
- Close emotional relationships disappear as all parties build up their protective walls.
- Sex life disappears.
- Social life suffers.
- Denial sets in as family members down play the seriousness of the situation.
- The family members may develop secondary trauma due to living in close proximity with the situation. The secondary PTSD comes from feeling the shock, pain, fear and anger at what happened to a loved one.
- Overprotection of the person with PTSD is not usually helpful but it does help to prevent the blow-ups...and so is done as a way to protect the family. This is not overly healthy but it sometimes works.

- Family trust disappears.
- The family becomes tense and anxious waiting for the next blow-up.
- Family members become over involved with their children's lives as they compensate for feeling lonely and require some positive emotional support. This over involvement may not be mentally healthy for the children as it could stifle normal independent development.
- In extreme cases physical abuse may be present.

What can the family do to help the person with PTSD?

It is just as important to know what you can't do as what you can do. You can't make the person get over PTSD. That has to come from within. Also you can't cheer up a person who is clinically depressed. Both of these situations require professional intervention.

You can be of assistance by:

- Learning what you can about PTSD, explaining as much as you can to the children of the family.
- Ensuring the person receives the required professional help.
- Trying to supply a loving and calm environment in the home.
- Letting the person talk about the events and how they see them.
- Never saying, "I know just how you feel." You don't and it will lessen your credibility in the eyes of the person who is trying to find his way.
- If you feel comfortable doing so you may want to help the person see the traumatic event in perspective.

- Trying to involve the person in discussions about day-to-day planning and plans for the future.
- Attempting to keep the person involved in a social life.
- Not letting yourself get run down or overwhelmed. You can't be of much help if you are worn out, resentful, angry or ready for an anxiety attack yourself.
- Notifying the counselor if you see signs of depression, suicide, anxiety or panic attacks, etc.

What can the family do to help themselves?
Read the chapters in this book regarding support people and how they may look after themselves. Look for other information from post-traumatic stress disorder groups. They may be obtained from your local mental health center, the Internet, veterans' associations and various departments of government.

- For your own sake learn as much as you can about PTSD
- It is my personal feeling the children in the family should be told as much as they can understand about PTSD. Not to do so could leave them feeling they are being ignored and unwanted by the person with the disorder.
- If applicable, attend courses for family members of those who suffer from alcoholism and/or addiction.
- Don't leave your job to look after the person. Apart from the money, contact with outside people is necessary as well as is your own feeling of self-worth.
- Don't give up your social life. You need others for a reality check.
- If any sign of violence or abuse occurs...get help immediately. That is not acceptable even if it is a symptom

of the disorder. Don't fall into the trap of feeling it was just a one time event or that the person did not mean it and won't do it again. With PTSD the person possibly did not mean it but there are ways that a person can deal with the anger other than taking it out on others.

- See a counselor yourself so you have someone to talk to. You can't keep the tension or numbness bottled up inside and expect to stay mentally and physically well.

Major Points

- Post-traumatic stress disorder is the result of some psychological trauma.
- It is related to anxiety disorders due to the fear of a reoccurrence of the event.
- Both those directly involved as well as those witnessing the event may be affected.
- There is no shame in developing PTSD. Anyone can develop it.
- PTSD may develop within a few weeks or not until years later. It may even disappear and reappear much later.
- Symptoms fall into various main groups including those caused by intrusive memories, avoidance of situations and other triggers that arouse anxiety.
- Guilt at not doing something to have prevented the event may be present—even if there was nothing the witness could have done.
- There is effective treatment for those with PTSD but the best treatment is one of prevention.

Seven

Obsessive–Compulsive Disorder

OBSESSIVE COMPULSIVE DISORDER (OCD) is a member of the anxiety group which affects about 2% of the population.

People with OCD are subjected to unwanted recurring thoughts, images or impulses that are almost always of a type which produce feelings of anxiety, fear or unease. "Some bad thing is going to happen if I don't do this." Sometimes they may know what they believe is going to happen (e.g. my parents will die), or it may an undefined bad event.

To reduce the anxiety these people develop actions or rituals that they feel they must perform in order to counteract the fears. To add to the anxiety they almost always know both the thoughts and their responding behavior are not rational. As with the other anxiety disorders, it can, if untreated, take over their whole day and has the potential to make some drastic unhealthy changes to the life of the family.

Let's look at some examples.

Ron can't leave any room without counting to 20 by twos. If he feels he has not got the cadence just right, he has to start again. Like many with OCD Ron has been able to cover up his need to count by intentionally dropping papers and pausing to pick them up, etc. Other people notice nothing wrong with him other than a tendency to be clumsy at times. He gets mad at himself because he knows it is all irrational..but he is compelled to do it anyway.

Andy is a baseball pitcher. Before each pitch he feels compelled to touch his belt three times. If he does not touch it just right he has to start again. Andy feels something bad will happen on the pitch if he does not do his touching. Why does the touching of the belt help Andy? He may not have any idea. The OCD was born out of some anxiety but the origin of relieving his feelings by touching his belt, he may not remember at all—if he ever knew. Perhaps at one time he had a zipper, which would not stay up. More likely he just subconsciously made up the patting to alleviate his anxious thoughts.

The above examples illustrate a number of points of OCD.

1. OCD is composed of two main components.
   - The obsession is the constant thought or worry that something bad will happen.
   - The compulsion is the act or ritual developed to counteract the obsession.
2. The obsessive thoughts produce an anxiety.

- The compulsive behavior is an attempt to lessen the anxiety

3. Those suffering from OCD know they are acting irrationally but the obsession is so strong there is little they can do about it other than go through the"neutralizing" ritual.

4. Many people are very good at covering up their compulsions. Ron just dropped papers so that he had time to do his counting correctly.

The examples we have looked at so far illustrate situations in which there is a single obsession present. Frequently there are several obsessions and compulsions which control the person's behavior and which can become so time consuming there is little time in the day for anything else.

Alicia is a person I came to know from a CHAT room on the Internet. I have used this discussion to help you understand the life of a person with OCD. Notice that even though she is very well informed she cannot, so far, control her thoughts and resulting actions to any great degree. Keep in mind that every person's private life with OCD is different. This is hers.

Alicia: "Hi ken! Thanks for dropping in. Alicia gives you a bear H U G !!!!!"

Ken: "HI"

Alicia: "Hello."

Ken: "Hugs to you too."

Alicia: "I read about half of your new chapter on OCD."

Ken: "Yes..."

Alicia: "I think it's great so far. Certain things

were mentioned that I never knew were OCD related."

Ken: "Oh, I am glad you found it useful. Thanks. It makes me want to finish the chapter. What did you find?"

Alicia: "Well the pulling of the hair and so on. I did it for over a year and a half. I did that as a young child."

Alicia: "Till my Mom spanked me for doing so."

Ken: "Did that stop you?"

Alicia: "Not at first. I think another compulsion or ritual took over."

Ken: "Some pull out eyebrows and anything else on their head."

Alicia: 'Well, when I think one of my rituals are under control, another one surfaces."

Alicia: "How much time do you have right now?"

Ken: "A few minutes."

Alicia: "Ok, I'll try to make this quick."

Ken: "Take your time."

Ken: "I meant I am in no great hurry."

Alicia: "I have checking rituals."

Ken: "..."

Alicia: "Such as, doors, windows, check if someone is breathing."

Ken: "Can be time consuming."

Alicia: "Yes, very time consuming."

Alicia: "And if the doors to the car or truck are closed."

Ken: "You keep checking to see that they are locked, the person is alive, etc.?"

Alicia: "Yes I do."

Ken: "Found a way to control them?"

Alicia: "No."

Alicia: "Another one was lyrics to a song."

Alicia: "That was another one I didn't know of."

Alicia: "Like you mentioned in your chapter."

Ken: "Just kept going through your head?"

Alicia: "Yes like a broken record."

Alicia: "I wanted to scream like a lunatic."

Ken: "You have some new things to talk over with your therapist."

Alicia: "Sorry to say this but he's not worth much."

Ken: "Have you been with this one long?"

Alicia: "About three years."

Ken: "Then find another. If you don't have confidence in your therapist you may not make much progress."

Alicia nods.

Alicia: "I need to."

Alicia: "I go to an OCD support group, It's a real good group."

Ken: "Good. I am glad it is a good group."

Alicia: "I would like to change therapists but most want money. Which I don't have since I'm on SSI for my disorders."

Ken: "Being in Canada, I don't know what SSI is?"

Alicia: "Disability like social security when a person is no longer able to work or function properly."

Ken: "Have you asked in you group about other therapists?"

Alicia: "No, not yet."

Ken: "Do others on this CHAT group know about your OCD?"

Alicia: "Some know but they don't understand."

Ken: "You have tried to explain to some on here?"

Alicia: "Yes I have mentioned to some in here. It's just they think I'll get over it somehow."

Ken: "I hope you will but as you know a 100% cure is not common. Much of the time you just reach the point where you can control the obsessions."

Alicia: "I'm aware of that."

Ken: "It is a very difficult disorder to understand."

Alicia: "I agree it's very difficult to understand."

Alicia: "Also, when the salt container falls I freak out. I think something bad is going to happen. So I pray for a very long time."

Alicia: "If a knife falls I feel the same. So I make a cross with the knife exactly where the knife has fallen."

Ken: "And that neutralized the feeling?"

Alicia: "To some degree, yes."

Ken: "Does one cross do it?"

Alicia: "About three times for me will do it."

Alicia: "I find myself saying prayers in my sleep."

Ken: "Praying for what?"

Alicia: "I guess my mind goes into over load when I finally get some sleep. So even my rituals follow me there. So I pray there also."

Ken: "You taking any meds?"

Alicia: "Yes."

Ken: "Do they help?"

Alicia: "None specifically for OCD."

Ken: "Many for anxiety also work for OCD."

Alicia: "Celexa is for depression, but it's known to help OCD. I'm glad it has helped me a bit."

Ken: "Yes, I have seen it mentioned."

Ken: "Do you belong to any OCD mail list?"

Alicia: "No I don't."

Ken: "They work for some people but not all."

Ken: "Does OCD run in your family?"

Alicia: 'I think my Mom had it.'

Ken: "You sleep by yourself don't you?"

Alicia: "My poodle sleeps with me."

Alicia: "But he needs to be very clean. If not I don't let him."

Alicia: "I also have contamination fears."

Alicia: "As a child I wasn't allowed to get dirty."

Alicia: "I won't use public phones or restrooms."

Ken: "What about the toilet after others use it?"

Alicia: "Well, I don't touch anything. Excuse my bluntness I squat, then flush the toilet with my foot."

Ken: "This is your own toilet?"

Alicia: "No, if I ever need to use a public bathroom."

Alicia: "I clean my toilet to death so it's not an issue."

Ken: "How about your own if you have company?"

Alicia: "I clean it when they leave, or I don't use it while their here."

Ken: "I understand."

Alicia: "I wash my hands a lot. Take baths or showers twice a day."

Ken: "Are you being asked to try to expose yourself to these things?"

Alicia: "No."

Alicia: "The people in the group are trying to suggest I do."

Ken: "Yes, it seems to work."

Alicia: "I know that's why I need another therapist."

Ken: "Maybe you should ask your therapist why he has not suggested it."

Alicia: "I notice I clean a lot when others come over. I feel it's also avoidance somehow."

Ken: "Avoidance of what?"

Alicia: "Being around others because they're invading my space."

Alicia: "Avoidance when I'm angry."

Ken: "This is OCD or anxiety?"

Alicia: "OCD."

Ken: "Actually, so a psychologist in Australia told me, there are very blurred boundaries between many of the anxiety disorders.'

Alicia nods.

Alicia: "I also have a thing about knives."

Ken: "What?"

Alicia: "I feel I will hurt someone or myself."

Alicia: "With knives."

Ken: "You mean deliberately?"

Alicia: "It's just recurring thoughts."

Alicia: "I've never acted on them."

Ken: "Yes, I understand that. And people with these types of feelings don't hurt themselves usually."

Ken: "It is rather like a person with no OCD being on a high cliff and getting the feeling they want to jump."

Alicia nods.

Alicia: "Also since I was molested and raped…"

Ken: "I am sorry. I did not know you were."

Alicia: "I never told anyone."

Ken: "I hope you told the cops."

Alicia: "No I didn't."

Alicia: "That's when my anxiety started when I was 4 or 5 years of age."

Ken: "When you were molested at 4 or 5. Were your parents involved?"

Alicia: "Oh dear God no! I had very good parents."

Ken: "Good."

Alicia: "So I don't think of kids that way. I just feel like I sexually offended others such as adults."

Alicia: "I think 'hmm, did I touch his butt.' I know I didn't touch it but I'm left wondering."

Ken: "Sorry, I don't understand."

Alicia: "I feel like I sexually offended someone even though I know in my heart I didn't."

Alicia: "This pertains to adults."

Ken: "Can you give me an example? Ken the dense."

Alicia: "It's very hard because I'm very affectionate."

Alicia: "For instance I have male friends. When I see them or visit them we hug and kiss. Later when I leave I ask myself did I grab his butt and so on. Was I sexually offensive?"

Ken: "You worry about what you might have done."

Alicia nods frantically!

Alicia: "I have to call them just to see how they react and be assured in some way I was ok."

Alicia: "I make an excuse and say sorry I was a sap and they say don't worry you were fine."

Ken: "So they understand?"

Alicia: "I'm not sure I think it's OCD related. I hear others' fear of hurting others. So they call them to see if they didn't hurt them somehow."

Ken: "You start off with a little idea and slowly your mind builds it up into a huge problem."

Alicia nods frantically!

Alicia: "I'm not sure if they understand. I don't come out and say why I asked or called them after leaving."

Ken: "Maybe it is. You obsess about having offended them?"

Alicia: "Yes I obsess about having offended them somehow."

Alicia: "I have many issues with OCD."

Ken: "It sound like you do."

Alicia: "I wanted to say thanks for listening."

Ken: "Thanks for telling me all this. I understand you much better."

Alicia: "Aww, thanks."

Alicia: "I also want this to stay private."

Ken: "Of course it will. I never say anything."

Alicia: "It's real hard. I have so many disorders overlapping."

Ken: "Can I change the name and use your experiences for the OCD chapter?"

Ken: "In this book?"

Alicia: "Sure. No problem."

Ken: "Thanks.'

Alicia: 'Did you write them down?"

Ken: "I still have them on my screen I will just copy them over."

Alicia: "Oh, ok."

Alicia: "Oh, thanks again."

Alicia: "If you have questions please don't hesitate to ask."

Alicia: "I feel very comfortable chatting with you."

Ken: "Thanks. I am glad you do."

Alicia: "Sorry I took up so much of your time."

Ken: "No, you didn't. I found it useful myself."

Alicia: "Ok."

Ken: "Good night."

Alicia: 'Night."

Alicia seems to be saying she is relating the OCD to sexual assault. However, it is generally recognized that having experienced sexual assault does not cause OCD or particular types of OCD, for example, sexual obsessions. I am not negating her feelings, just making a general comment.

A very striking example of OCD involves that of Howard Hughes. Hughes was well known and respected for his work in aviation and movie production. In later years he had become a recluse but people were stunned when, upon his death in 1976, it was discovered many rooms of his large house were crammed with his nail clippings and hair snippings as well as innumerable bottles of urine. He just could not throw them out.

Now you have a background in OCD let's move on to some specific types of behavior.

Hoarding

Some things are never discarded. Garbage, newspapers, pieces of string, old clothing, etc. "They might come in useful someday." "I might throw out something I need." "My mother may die if I throw these out."

Apart from running out of room, hoarding can become a health hazard. A number of years ago I was dropping something at the home of one of my 17-year-old students. When the door opened the stench was appalling. Every place that I could see was piled with leaking garbage bags. I quietly had a word with our school nurse. When the student graduated a few months later I asked how things were at home. She said her mother had finally got rid of all the garbage but the compulsion had been replaced by a need to record all the nature shows on TV. Her mother had 3 VCR's and was constantly checking both the printed schedule and the timers on the VCR's to ensure she had them programmed correctly. It is not uncommon in OCD to find that when one compulsion is overcome it is replaced by another.

In another situation I was invited into a home which was stacked high with so many piles of newspapers it was impossible to sit down or even move about a room. The house had a water problem and the papers gave off so many fungal spores I found it difficult to breathe.

Constant Counting

This is done in one's head. How many tiles in the ceiling, how many steps across a room. How many power poles in a city block. Repetitively counting the buttons in a box.

Jeremy was a slow reader but he understood what he read. It did not come out until much later that Jeremy was counting the number of letters in each word that he read.

Obsessive Neatness

Objects must be arranged in a certain very neat manner. Hours can be spent getting them just right.

Maxine was a person who could not stand one piece of litter on her small townhouse lawn. All through the year she spent most of her waking hours removing leaves as soon as they fell to the lawn. She did not even have peace during the winter as one of the trees was an arbutus which is an evergreen and drops either leaves or bark shreds almost throughout the entire year.

Another situation involved a man who wrote that he would get the screaming mi mi's as he waited in the car for his wife who could not leave the house unless the pony tails on the rugs were exactly lined up. Many times when she opened the door to finally leave, a breeze would nudge some slightly out of line so it was back to square one.

Having to Do Things a Certain Number of Times or in a Certain Order

Things must be done in groups of threes. Three knocks on the door; shower three times. (It can by any number…just happened to be 3s in the examples.)

Bodily Functions and Anatomy

Some people constantly check their body and body functions. They will check to see if they can find any hint of a developing disease.

At the age of 18 Lorna was taught how to do self-breast examinations looking for tumors. Soon she was doing it several times a day. Other people will be concerned if they are producing enough urine or worrying that a pimple may be the onset of skin cancer. Another person I heard from had been diagnosed with Type II diabetes. She felt compelled to test her blood sugar several times an hour.

It is not uncommon for these people to be visiting doctor after doctor looking for reassurance about one thing or the other.

Excessive Fear of Germs or Contamination

There can an obsession with germs or chemical poisoning. Surgical gloves or masks may be worn. Hands are washed until they are raw then washed again.

Scott became obsessed with picking up germs from almost anything. His fear, of course, was that he would become ill. The compulsive behaviors he developed over the years brought him to a grinding halt in gridlock. At first he just wore gloves, then a mask and from here moved on to completely covering his skin with clothes that even he would not touch. He was so afraid to touch anything he would just stand around most of the day, even afraid to sit. Someone had to dress and undress him. Only canned food was eaten and then it had to be opened in his presence. Sheets and pillowcases had to be changed every time he woke up. By now his wife and family had long gone. Instead of the loss of his family being a huge wake-up call he was able to carry on as his mother moved right in and was happy to have her little boy back as she continued to help him continue with his OCD. The term for helping the person continue with their problems is "enabling." His mother was just happy to have got that other woman out of his life and would do anything to keep him needing her. It is an understatement to suggest she had problems too.

Revulsive or Disturbing Thoughts or Mind Pictures

These are recurring thoughts or pictures, which come into the mind and are very disturbing or repugnant to the person experiencing them. Even though the person has no intention of carrying them out they are disturbed that they could even think of them. These could involve bizarre sexual acts, hurting themselves or others, etc.

Not too long ago a story appeared in the media about a woman who had been diagnosed with OCD and had mentioned to someone she had these terrifying thoughts of hurting the baby she was now carrying. The story also mentioned that she had stopped her medication as soon as she found out she was pregnant as she felt it may be harmful to the baby. Word of her obsessive thoughts got back to the local government authorities and, through an apparent ignorance of OCD, somehow it was suggested she must have Munchausen's Syndrome by Proxy and the baby was removed from her care at birth. Eventually it was sorted out but the trauma to the parents was great. (Munchausen's Syndrome by Proxy is a rare disorder in which parents, usually the mother, fabricate symptoms in their children, thus subjecting the child to unnecessary medical tests and/or surgical procedures. In some cases, the parents may also inflict injury on the child to strengthen the stories.)

Nonsense Words or Songs That Keep Going Through the Head

Ever had the words from a song keep going around in

your head for a few hours? It can be annoying yet you can't cut them off. That is a very small taste of what can occur in the mind of a person with OCD. They just can't cut them off and they may, with breaks of varying intervals, keep going around for months if not longer. *"Diddley-do, Diddley-do, Diddley Diddley, Diddly-Do. Diddley-do, Diddley-do, Diddley Diddley, Diddly-Do. Diddley-do, Diddley-do, Diddley Diddley, Diddly-Do." (Shut up! Stop it!) "Diddley-do, Diddley-do, Diddley Diddley, Diddly-Do. Diddley-do, Diddley-do, Diddley Diddley, Diddly-Do. (God! Help me to stop!) Diddley-do, Diddley-do, Diddley Diddley, Diddly-Do."* ...and so on *ad infinitum*.

Constant Checking. Doubting What They Had Just Seen with Their Own Eyes

Constantly checking light switches, the stove or, the cat to see if is still breathing. It may start off as a need to constantly assure themselves that there is no problem with the item, but it might rapidly develop into a life of its own as a person has to touch the stove switches to ease the fear of some vaguely defined bad thing happening.

Peter had checked the thermostat was turned down at least six times before he and his family went out the door. Half way down the steps he turned around, unlocked the door, and checked it just one more time. On the way to town he kept asking if he had checked the thermostat and that maybe they should go back and look again. His wife behaved correctly in not responding to him and certainly in not turning the car around. she assured him once that he had turned it down and refused to talk about it further.

The French common name for OCD is "The Doubting Disease." That makes sense.

Constant Reassurance

The requirement of constant assurance may also be a symptom of OCD. Are you sure we are on the right road? Are you sure I have changed the tire correctly? Are you sure the accountant said I had filled out the forms correctly?

Ruth and Darren had just boarded the plane for their honeymoon. Ruth kept asking if he was sure their luggage had been tagged to the same place they were going. Darren kept assuring her that he had watched and they had been tagged correctly. Ruth then started asking if he had checked their reservations. After some time of this Darren became a bit annoyed and asked what the problem was. Ruth was then faced the decision of:

a. telling him the truth that the OCD she had thought was under control and so had not mentioned to him had flared up probably because of the stress of the wedding or

b. remaining silent and hope she could keep it under control.

As you will see later, OCD is rarely completely cured but it can be kept under control and may just pop up in times of stress.

Being Scrupulously Correct

There are several letters on the internet about people who have the obsession of being scrupulously correct.

A frequent example given is that of a person who goes to Confession but is never sure they have mentioned all the sins committed. Some of them will make several trips a day because they remembered something else.

Obsessions Without Compulsions

Sometimes people have frequent disturbing thoughts, which are not associated with any actions.

> Barbara was frightened. She had frequent images of herself holding a large shiny knife ready to stab someone. Barb knew she would never hurt anyone and had no urges to do so.

(These people don't hurt others. They are just afraid they will.)

Compulsions Without Obsessions

> As Dale walked down a street he had a need to touch every telephone pole he passed. There was no feeling of something bad would happen...he just had to do that.

Close Cousins of OCD

Some professionals include these in with OCD and others relate them indirectly and some insist they are not related at all.

Tricotillomania

Hair pullers. Those suffering from this disorder have a compulsion to pull out hair from their head, eyebrows and any other location on their bodies. It is usually done one strand at a time and may become so bad that a wig may be worn to hide it.

Dysmorphophobia

People suffering from dysmorphophobia are normal looking in all respects but become obsessed with the idea that something is wrong with their appearance. Their nose may be far too large; they feel their face is ugly. Much of their day may be spent looking at reflections of themselves. Some will feel they are so "deformed' they will not venture outdoors or allow themselves to be seen by anyone but the immediate family.

Nymphomania and its male counterpart satyriasis

These disorders result in excessive sexual behavior and gratification. At one time some researchers included these disorders with OCD. That is no longer the case. They are now classified as impulse disorders. In included them here for two reasons.

1. To ensure people who have obtained their information from older tests are now aware that nymphomania and satyriasis are not a form of OCD.

2. To clearly spell out that people with OCD do not do anything that will harm others. As seen in the conversation with Alicia, they are sometimes afraid they may do something improper or harmful—but they don't.

Treatment of OCD

It has been estimated by a number of OCD clinics that in adults it takes 5 to 8 years from the noticing of the first symptoms to the time treatment is sought. This delay is probably due to a number of factors:

• The first symptoms are so slight they are not really noticed and may just exist in the person's head as obsessions without compulsions.

- The build-up and development of the obsessions may develop so slowly they are not noticed until someone finally has had enough and demands the person stop the activity or go get some help.
- Resistance to treatment due to denial on the part of the person with OCD.
- The relative personality strengths of the members of the family. If the person with OCD is the "dominant' member of the family, the other members may go along with it. Children, however, do tend to question the unusual behavior which they do not see in other homes.
- Shame on the part of the family. They do not want knowledge of the problem to get past walls of the house.
- Fear on the part of the other adult who feels trapped but has nowhere to go.
- Lack of support from other family members and people at work who have not seen the behavior. Some people with OCD are very adept at hiding the symptoms outside of the house.
- Fear on the part of the person with OCD. For example, this letter from ex-sufferer, Bob explains his feelings at the time:

"Sure, I wanted to get better and I took my pills but when it came to behavior therapy I could not do it. I was afraid that I would have to start giving up the anxiety reducing actions I was using. There was no way I could see myself getting dressed without going through my 'rituals'. The idea was just too stressful for me to pursue."

Bob is not alone in being afraid of letting go of his stress reducing compulsions. Several writers equate it to the same type of fear an alcoholic feels when trying to decide to get help.

For the treatment of OCD the first stop is frequently the family physician. He will probably recommend a psychologist or psychiatrist who has had success treating the disorder. Names of specialists may be obtained through local hospitals, the psychology and psychiatry departments of universities as well from your local mental health facilities. Some libraries keep the names of local support groups for both the person with OCD and for the family.

The sooner treatment is started the better. Unfortunately, as you have seen, it may take some time for the person or the family to realize there is a serious problem. Treatment should definitely be sought by the time the disorder begins to interfere with everyday life. Hopefully a wider awareness of OCD and other anxiety disorders will lead to treatment being sought sooner.

Research and time have shown that a combination of medication and behavioral therapy has been the most effective in patients. The exact type of treatment will depend upon such various factors as age, severity, length of time with the disorder or preference of the professional in charge of the treatment. Should there be more than one professional working with the patient, every effort should be made to ensure they are working together and not in isolation. For instance a psychiatrist may be administering medication while a psychologist is attending to the behavioral therapy. Also, there is no harm whatsoever in seeking a second opinion or asking for a change of medication if, after a reasonable length of time, the drugs do not seem to be working.

OCD can be a very stubborn disorder to treat. In many cases do not expect a 100% lifetime cure. It may disappear for a period of time then return or it may drop down to a level where the person is able to control the compulsions. Hopefully, the end result will be a controlled situation that may be symptom free for a long time and, when it does pop its head up, it can be swatted down so it develops into nothing more than a few rumblings of its former self.

After the Therapy Program is Completed

Hopefully the person will continue to be able to ignore the obsessive thoughts and take steps immediately to swat them back down should they start to arise again.

Medication may be required for long periods after the program but that is really nothing worse than a person who has thyroid problems having to take thyroxin the rest of her life is.

To the Support People to Those with Obsessive–Compulsive Disorder

Like a number of the other anxiety disorders OCD can, if allowed to, upset the family and produce feelings of loss, confusion, helplessness, despair, or worse.

The following section is based on extracts from *...Nine, Ten, Do It Again: A Guide to Obsessive–Compulsive Disorder.* 2nd edition, 1997. The author, Kathryn I'Anson is the Director of the Obsessive–Compulsive & Anxiety Disorders Foundations of Victoria (Australia). The material has been reproduced by kind permission of the author. The British and Australian term for "support person" is "carer."

Helping the Carer

If you are a spouse, sibling, mother, father, child or friend of a person who has OCD, then it is quite possible that you have been suffering too. Carers of people with OCD have to deal with many emotions that arise as a consequence of living with and caring for a sufferer. You are likely to feel worried, frustrated and confused, and sometimes despairing. These difficult feelings arise from the impact of the OCD on your relationship and environment and because it is so hard to see someone close to you either battling or in despair over thoughts and behaviors that seem to make no sense. Maybe insidious guilt thoughts creep into your mind. "Is it my fault?" "What have I done wrong?" "Should I have loved and cared for him/her more?" Maybe you feel angry and confused—simply can't understand how it is possible that this person, who seems quite rational in all other respects, just can't stop these ridiculous behaviors. Have you secretly wondered, "Is it attention seeking, laziness, naughtiness?" On top of all these conflicting feelings, there is the feeling of helplessness; you just don't know what to do.

The Following Ideas and Strategies May Help

Do not condemn yourself for having negative feelings. They are natural reactions to a difficult and confusing illness. You cannot be expected to understand behaviors and emotions that you have not experienced yourself—at least initially. You will develop greater understanding if you spend time reading relevant material and listening to your family member and other sufferers at support groups. However, negative feelings will continue to arise—occasionally or often, and self-condemnation and guilt over these feelings will only make them more difficult to let go. Accept your feelings, and actively find a way of releasing them on a daily basis—for example, talk them through with a friend, cry, go for a long walk or drive, do an activity such as gardening, painting or craft which enables the creative expression of feeling.

Obtain Support and Care for Yourself
Maybe you have a great circle of family and friends who provide an empathic listening ear and practical help when you need it. If not, you might consider joining your local OCD Support Group where you will find some people to care for you, and you can talk to and learn from other carers who have been in similar situations.

If your own state of mental and emotional health is suffering, it may be helpful for you to see a therapist. This will be a positive act of affirmation that your health and needs are important, and will put you in a better position to help the sufferer effectively.

Obtain and Read Information and Books About OCD So that the Disorder Can Be Put into a Proper Perspective
As you learn more, you will be able to make some new choices about your feeling and reactions to the OCD. For example, you will learn that your family member's strange and exces-

sive behaviors are not caused by a lack of willpower, and that pleading, threatening or cajoling them to stop will not help. You will learn to accept that the OCD impulsive urge, anxiety and intrusive thoughts are the compelling force behind the repetitive behaviors, the slowness, the constant questions or requests for reassurance. You will also learn that you didn't cause it. You will recognize the important part you can play in your family member's recovery and discover many ways that you can help. The recovery journey will not be easy and you will still feel frustrated and despairing sometimes. However, now you know why you are feeling this way, and that your feelings are a reaction to the OCD, not the sufferer.

Take Some Time Out for Yourself

Every week—or every day if possible, spend some time doing something that you really enjoy and where you cannot be interrupted. We all need some time to ourselves, and we all need time to relax, have fun, and to pursue those goals that interest us. If you are able to look after you own mental and emotional well-being, you will cope better with the stresses that the OCD brings into you life.

Helping The Sufferer

If you have been living with a family member who has had severe OCD for along period of time, it is likely that the disorder has caused significant disruption and distress to your home life, relationships and social life. Possibly you have been involved in the sufferer's rituals or avoidance behaviors, trying to ease her distress, or just to keep the peace.

Avoidance Behaviors

People with OCD avoid many situations or objects that trigger their compulsions. Your involvement in avoidance behaviors may take many forms—for example, you may do all the shopping because the sufferer's compulsions are triggered by contamination and decision making fears involved with buying food; or you may always have to cook the meals, clean the house, or answer the home telephone or the front door because of similar triggers of compulsions and the sufferer becomes too distressed if pressed to these things. There are several things that you can do to help ease the daily stresses and aid the sufferer in their recovery.

Share Your Knowledge and New Understanding of the Disorder with the Sufferer

The isolation that your family member has been feeling has been an enormous burden, and she has been feeling distressed and guilty about the affect of the disorder on you. Now, hopefully, you will both be able to talk about the disorder, and express your feelings about it, openly and honestly. This will be a great beginning to the healing process for both of you, and any other family members of friends that are involved.

Encourage the Sufferer to Talk to You About Her Disorder

This will help you to understand exactly how her obsessions and compulsions, have been interwoven into the daily fabric of her life, an yours. This

may be very difficult for as it is often very embarrassing and to explain, so ask, but don't push and
let her tell you in her own time. When your family member does decide to confide in you, listen
attentively, encourage her to get it all out, and
thank her for trusting you. Return this trust by
accepting what she tells you as an honest and
accurate account of what she feels and experiences. Ask questions, if you need to, to clarify
what the anxiety or compulsion or obsession is
and when it occurs, but don't start trying to
engage the sufferer in discussion about the logic
her behaviors. The sufferer will immediately
catch on to the fact that you do not understand,
and it may be a long time before she will confide
in you again.

**Encourage the Sufferer to Obtain Professional
Help**
Your role here will be to provide support and
encouragement and, if she agrees, to offer some
practical help in locating an experienced therapist. If the sufferer decided to try behavior therapy, and if you have been extensively involved in
the rituals or avoidance behaviors, it will be
important that you join in the therapy at some
stage. The sufferer will need your help as she
begins doing the work with exposure and
response prevention, and so you will need to
know what to do, what not to do, and the best
ways to support her. If you and other members of
the family are involved in the sufferer's rituals or
avoidance behaviors it is important that you

begin to reduce your involvement and find ways of normalizing the family routines.

Firstly, discuss this with the sufferer—don't just abruptly stop your involvement as this may cause her a great deal of agonizing distress. Tell her that you want to reduce your part in the rituals or avoidance behaviors to help her get better, and decide with her which ones you and other family members will no longer participate in. Set some realistic goals together, and make sure that the whole family agrees to abide by the plan. Once you begin to work co-operatively together in this way, your situation will gradually change and the sufferer will no longer take your involvement for granted. When the sufferer undertakes behavior therapy or a self-help program, the work you have done together will give her a great head start. Once therapy begins— whether pharmacotherapy" [medication] "or behavior therapy, your involvement in the sufferer's rituals and avoidance behaviors should be reduced to zero—if at all possible. The doctor or therapist will need to be informed if your involvement continues, so that they can work on this aspect with the sufferer.

Create a Supportive Home Environment
The home is often the primary setting of compulsions, and is also generally the 'haven of avoidance' for the anxiety sufferer. The less tension that in 'in the air' the better. If there are significant conflicts in some the family relationships, it would be very helpful to the sufferer if these con-

flicts are worked through and resolved—including those conflicts that include the sufferer.

Ask your family member to tell you when she is having a particularly hard day.

Your family member's symptoms may flare up when her anxiety is high, she is depressed, or when she is stressed about something. Offer what support you can, and be flexible in terms of what you are expecting from the sufferer on that day.

If you notice improvements, however small, acknowledge them, and encourage the sufferer to reward themselves for the progress. For example cutting down a hand washing routine by 5 minutes, or reducing a checking ritual from 50 checks to 40 checks may seem insignificant, but represents a great step forward by the sufferer. Your recognition and praise will encourage her to keep trying.

Try to maintain a non-judgmental and accepting attitude toward the sufferer. A non-judgmental attitude from you and all the family, to sufferer, and avoidance or personal criticism, will enable the sufferer to focus her efforts at coping and getting well, rather than expending her efforts in dealing with anger and resentment.

Laughter is Good Medicine
When the sufferer is doing well, and having a good day, a bit of humor and laughter—offered with sensitivity, is great balm to soothe away some of the painful feelings and thought which arise.

Be Patient

None of the treatments or self-help programs that are available for sufferers provide quick "cures"—or even immediate relief. Recovery is a slow and gradual process. Be prepared to support the sufferer on a long-term recovery program, and don't make day-to-day comparisons. Recovery always includes slips and setbacks—the important thing is that the setback isn't interpreted as failure. The guilt and stress that will arise from thoughts and feelings of failure could make the set-back much more difficult to overcome, than if it is viewed as an opportunity to learn.

There can be no simple, straightforward plan that will smooth away every rock on the road to recovery. Every person who has OCD, and every family who has a sufferer as a member, has a different set of symptoms and circumstances to deal with, different relationships, different personalities and a whole complex array of different influences. Try these ideas and strategies, and draw upon all the resources and support that you have. Slowly, but surely, you and the sufferer will discover the treatments and self-help strategies and ideas that will work for you."

As Kathryn I'Anson mentioned above, humor is one method to help the caregivers. Sandy is a woman who tried to deal with her husband's OCD through humor. She put up a mock ad on an OCD message board to which she belonged.

> **WILL TRADE HUSBAND FOR 1 WEEK**
> Wanted, a husband with OCD who suffers from excessive neatness. Will trade for a husband who is a hoarder. At the end of the week I figure both houses should sort of be back to a normal state of affairs.

Main Points

1. OCD is composed of two main components.
   - The obsession is the constant thought or worry something bad will happen.
   - The compulsion is the act or ritual developed to counteract the obsession.
2. The obsession thoughts produce an anxiety. The compulsive behavior is an attempt to lessen the anxiety.
3. Those suffering from OCD know they are acting irrationally.
4. Many people are very good at covering up their compulsions.
5. OCD can exist in many forms and many degrees of severity.
6. This is classified as an anxiety disorder as the obsessions produce the anxiety. The sufferers seek to reduce the anxiety through the rituals they have made up.
7. Compulsions also reinforce and maintain anxiety and obsessions.

8. Treatment frequently consists of medication and behavioral therapy.

9. If one obsession is overcome, the disorder may continue to manifest itself through another obsession. Remember the person who had the house full of newspapers. He finally was convinced to discard the newspapers. Then he turned to taping every nature show he could find on TV.

10. As caregivers there few main points of which you should be aware:

- Do not take part in any of the OCD behavior.

- Do not allow the OCD behavior to upset the house routine.

- Watch to see you are not part of their avoidance behavior. For instance, if a person's triggers include shopping they may always find an excuse to not go so you have to go instead.

- The general suggestions for caregivers found in Chapter 14 also apply.

Eight

Methods of Treatment

THIS BRIEF SECTION has been included to give you a basic understanding of the method of treatment the person you are with may be undergoing. There are several methods used. Some may be used on their own, while frequently, more than one method is used at the same time. Since this is a book for caregivers, I am not advocating any particular method that is a matter for discussion with professionals. Also, I have not gone into detail here, because there are several books available on these techniques. As a support person you may wish to consult books on these methods.

The relaxation techniques can be just as useful to you. Give them a try—perhaps do them together.

Cognitive Behavioral Therapy

This form of treatment is a combination of behavioral and cognitive therapy. It is a very commonly used tech-

nique for anxiety disorders. The thinking patterns are
changed to accept and roll with the anxiety. The person
learns to understand what is going on and slowly work
her way back into anxious situations.

Behavioral Therapy

The fear must be faced before it can be overcome.
Desensitization occurs by being *in* the situation. This is
frequently approached with baby steps.

Cognitive Therapy

Your thoughts and attitude are responsible for the way
in which you respond to an event. This technique
requires a person to change the way they look at things.
My glass is half full vs. my glass is half empty. The negative self-talk is replaced by positive self-talk. Change
the "What ifs" to "So whats."

Interceptive Exposure

An individual purposely brings on bodily sensations
that are similar to those experienced during panic
episodes so that they have the opportunity to learn
they are not dangerous (e.g., spinning to bring on dizziness, rapid breathing to bring on light-headedness and
dry mouth, wearing a tie tightly around the neck to
bring on a tight throat, etc).

Naturalistic Exposure

Used for the same purpose as interceptive exposure.
Examples include drinking caffeinated coffee or running up stairs to bring on rapid heart rate, etc.

Support Therapy

Primarily talking about a problem or situation and suggestions being made.

Medications

See Chapter 9.

Meditation, Tai Chi, Calming Music, etc.

Slow the mind; become more centered and focused.

Prayer

This has been very helpful for many.

Visualization

Seeing yourself doing it before actually doing it. This is rather similar to what some athletes do before entering the event.

Virtual Reality

Computer generated graphics allow a person to "walk" through a place or a situation which causes anxiety prior to actually doing it.

Relaxation Techniques

Getting the slow-down system going. Several books and tapes are available for the various techniques. Why not try this and some of the other methods yourself? You need to relax too.

Developing Coping Strategies

Things to do when the anxiety level is very high. This

"arsenal" is extremely important in keeping the anxiety under control and not letting it "blow out."

Diet

Some people find certain foods such as sugar and caffeine can increase their anxiety level.

Exercise

Regular exercise of even 10 to 20 minutes a day has been shown to be helpful in reducing anxiety and well as depression.

Exorcisms

These have not been used much for mental disorders for the past 200 or 300 years. They are a bit out of vogue. However, one woman I had communicated with for several weeks finally told me why she would not seek treatment. Her doctor had advised a psychiatrist while her church insisted she be exorcised. When it comes to religious matters I maintain my silence. However, in this case, I suggested she go with her doctor's advice. A couple of weeks later she wrote to me very upset. If I understand it correctly, because I had suggested she take her doctor's advice and not the exorcism, the rector of her church insisted I must be acting as an agent of the devil and the congregation was praying for the damnation of my soul. Oh well. Goes with the territory I suppose. No, I have not lost any sleep over it. It so happened that at the time I was being branded an agent of the devil, I was on my church's council.

Eye Movement Desensitization and Reprocessing

A fairly new technique that seems to show promise for some.

Thought Field Therapy

TFT is a brief therapy technique used to treat anxiety, post-traumatic stress disorders, phobias and grief. It is also used in the treatment of depression and pain management. While TFT is not well known, there are some in our group who say it has worked for them.

Alternative Medical Treatments

These methods include herbs, homeopathy, vitamins, etc.

Many of the methods given above have been used successfully for some time. Several are used with trained counselors and others can be self-initiated. As the support person, you can also take advantage of one or more of the self initiated programs to keep your energy level up and stress level down.

How successfully the individual techniques work depends upon a number of factors (severity, how long they have had the disorder, type of disorder, etc.) The results vary from person to person. The suggestions given in this book for support people are general and most are applicable to almost all of the anxiety disorders as well as the type of treatment being used.

Some clinics specialize in taking selected people and working with them for a week to so. During this week they are prepared for the virtual total immersion in situations that bring on panic attacks. Baby steps are not used.

Another form of therapy is to do exercises that bring on the symptoms of panic attacks. The symptoms are then analyzed and explained in terms of what physiological events are occurring in the body. It is believed that such exposure to the symptoms and the understanding of them will allow the person to realize they are "normal" body symptoms, thus removing the fear caused by the symptoms. These would include racing heart, dizziness, etc.

To the Person You Are Supporting

If the method you are using works—great! Stick to it. If the method is not working it may be time for to try something else. Don't be discouraged. It is not you; it is the techniques. You may want to modify some of the techniques. If you are working with a counselor suggest changes to her. If you are on your own, show a bit of ingenuity.

Well, Since You Insist

While I deliberately do not advocate any particular method, I constantly receive questions about what method is used the most. That is hard to answer since it varies, but the one which is currently receiving the most interest is a combination of medications for a kick-start and cognitive behavioral therapy. Many professionals stress that even if the initial bout of anxiety/panic attacks seems to pass off almost on its own, a person should receive cognitive behavioral therapy treatment. Not to do so could see the disorder return at a later date and possibly worse.

Also, the sooner a bout of anxiety is treated, the faster and more permanently it will go away.

Nine

Medications

Any gathering of anxious people will undoubtedly produce questions on medications—such as these from the Internet.

- "I'm starting Inderal tomorrow. What can I expect?"
- "My doctor just gave me Elavil. Should I take it?"
- "I started Luvox 2 days ago and feel electric shocks. Is this normal?"
- "I don't believe in medications."
- "I'm frightened to take anything. I hear such terrible stories."
- "After that experience I won't try another drug."
- "My doctor wants me to change drugs but I don't want to."
- "I'm going to just quit that drug."
- "I'm taking Paxil and it turned my life around."
- "I'm now taking Wellbutrin and find myself much better. It wasn't the first drug I tried and it isn't the complete answer."

Some of the anti-anxiety drugs are very potent. Some of the drugs do produce severe side effects *in some people.* Some can be addictive. Some people take the drugs with very few or no side effects.

So which of the above statements are valid?

All of them. Let's take them one at a time.

"I don't believe in medications." Fair enough. It's their body and they have a perfect right to refuse the drugs. The problem here is that their type of anxiety may respond very well to one or more of the wide variety of relatively safe medications. The support person may want to ask a number of questions about why medications are refused so adamantly. What is the reason for the refusal? Is it based on fear of drugs or a philosophical/religious belief? Is the fear of swallowing involved? Is it a fear of giving up control of the body's chemistry to an outside force? Is it fair to themselves and to the family not to try the drugs? What will insurance companies do if the doctor reports that the patient is not following instructions? These questions have to be worked out at the family level but not in a way that adds to their stress, fear and guilt. (Who said you didn't have to have the wisdom of Solomon at times —and the patience of Job?)

"My doctor just gave me Elavil. Should I take it?"

Here they are going to be receiving feedback from several people. More than likely they are looking for reassurance, but whether or not they receive it depends upon the group they ask. When asking others for feedback on taking new drugs, it is likely that a variety of answers and contradictory experiences will be offered. If the decision is made not to take the drugs then the doctor should be notified. Perhaps the doctor has some other ideas or can alleviate the fears.

"I started Luvox 2 days ago and feel electric shocks. Is this normal?"
Again, the person is probably looking for reassurance that this is not some horrible unknown side effect. The doctor can give the assurance. Several inexpensive paperbacks are now available describing possible side effects. You should also know that anxious people are hyperaware of changes in body states e.g., a small change in heart beat pattern will be quickly noticed.

"I'm frightened to take anything. I hear such terrible stories."
Many drugs do have unwanted side effects. The doctor will probably mention some of the common ones as well as those that can be dangerous—if any. The doctor probably will not mention side effects which occur in only 1% or 5% of the people taking them.

So why do they hear such terrible stories? The side effects do occur; get a large enough group together and several people have either had the side effect or "know someone" who has. Couple this with the high anxiety level present in these people and it is a situation that, while very much a concern to them, is blown out of proportion. It does little good to cajole or ridicule; their fear is real. I have always made it a habit to be around for a while when a person starts a new drug.

Another aspect is that people with anxiety disease have lost some control over the way their bodies react and don't want to give up any more control by using drugs.

"After that experience I won't try another drug."
If a bad experience is had with one drug it is only natural that some fear will be involved in trying another

one. Again, I don't give them meaningless statements like, "Nothing will happen." You can't guarantee that. You can just promise to be present when they do start it. Some prefer to start off with a small piece of the tablet if the doctor agrees. However, don't push; many will come around to taking it in their own time. If not, there is little you can do. The final decision is theirs.

"My doctor wants me to change drugs but I don't want to."

Why does the doctor want them to change drugs? Is there something better out now or is insufficient progress being made with the current drug? Ask. If the person isn't capable of making sure they get a clear answer have them give the doctor permission to talk to you about it. It would be very helpful to find why the anxious person does not wish to change drugs. It may be a fear of reacting to something new or a psychological dependency on the current drug. Talk it out if you can—calmly. Don't expect to always receive entirely rational reasons. Remember the person may be acting from a fear base, not a rational base. That they may be acting from a fear base does not make the reason any less valid or less real to them.

"I'm going to just quit that drug."

No way! Get medical advice. Just stopping many of these drugs cold can have dangerous effects. It is also a good idea to keep a few weeks supply of the drug on hand at all times in case some natural disaster occurs which prevents the prescription being refilled when required.

"I'm taking Paxil and it turned my life around."

Most people do report some to a great deal of improvement with the prescriptions they have been given.

They take the medications and find positive effects with few, if any, uncomfortable side effects.

"I'm now taking Rivotril and find myself much better. It wasn't the first drug I tried and it isn't the complete answer." This is a more realistic situation. It may take a few attempts to find the correct drugs and dosages. And the drugs may alleviate the symptoms to give a jump-start to the necessary changes in thinking patterns.

Recognizing the problems in finding the correct drug, some pharmacies will give a person a few pills to try to see if they can be taken without problems. It is little use paying for expensive drugs if you just have to throw them out. For example, a local pharmacist in Victoria charges his fee up front on the first few pills but just charges the drug cost on filling the remainder of the prescription. Ask the pharmacist about this method or ask the doctor if he has any free samples.

The Medications

This is a very brief overview of the categories of the medications. More information can be obtained from the doctor or pharmacist.

As mentioned above, a number of the newer medications do not have the same problems associated with them, as did some of the older ones. New ones are constantly in development and coming on line.

I • Antidepressants

This group of drugs generally takes 2 to 6 weeks before the full benefit or potential is reached. They are used for treatment of anxiety, panic attacks, depression and obsessive-compulsive disorders.

1. Monoamine Oxidase Inhibitors (MAOI)

   Generally these are not used much today as they can react with some foods and nonprescription drugs to produce serious, if not fatal, rises in blood pressure. These drugs can, however, be highly effective and safe for those willing to follow the dietary restrictions. Examples: Nardil, Parnate.

2. Tricyclic Antidepressants (TCA)

   In Chapter One you read how the body is constantly keeping itself in balance. As part of this process norepinephrine (part of the slow down system) and serotonin (sort of a "feeling happy" chemical) are routinely taken out of action. The TCAs change the rate at which they are taken out of action. Due to side effects it may be necessary to try several different types of TCAs before a satisfactory combination of dosage and drug is found. Even so, tricyclics have been used safely for decades. Examples: Elavil, Tofranil.

3. Serotonic Specific Uptake Inhibitors also known as Selective Serotonic Reuptake Inhibitors (SSRI)

   Similar in action to the TCAs but, as the name suggests, they act on serotonin only. Examples: Prozac, Luvox, Paxil, Zoloft, Celexa.

4. There are a number of smaller groups of antidepressants that act in a manner similar to that of MAOIs and SSRIs. Examples: Manerix and Effexor.

II • Bendodiazepines
(Known as the minor tranquilizers)

This group includes some of the commonest anti-anxiety drugs prescribed today. They are fast acting, short lived in the body and used mostly for short periods of time as many tend to be physically addictive and, over time, the body may become adjusted to them so the dosage may have to be increased to continue to obtain the required results. Where, for various reasons, they may be used for longer periods at high dosages, it is important that they may be discontinued only under medical supervision.

As a result of this description some may think these drugs should be avoided but remember this group does include some of the most commonly prescribed anxiety drugs being taken by literally millions of people, so don't discard them out of hand.

Some examples: Xanax, Valium, Ativan

III • ß-Andrenergics (Beta-Blockers)

To make a complicated story simple, these drugs retard the effects of the "speed-up" system chemicals—adrenaline and adrenaline-like compounds. They are used for anxiety.

Example: Inderal.

IV • Other Categories

There are a number of other drugs which do not fit into the above categories. Their uses vary from anti-anxiety medication to antidepressants. Examples: Buspar, lithium, and other mood stabilizers.

Ten

Negative Thinking
Welcome to Spin City

NEGATIVE THINKING IS FREQUENTLY a component of the anxiety disorders. It is almost always present in depression. For spin doctoring very little can beat the mind of a person afflicted with negative thinking.

What is Negative Thinking?

Negative thinking is a destructive thought process that bans any positive, happy or satisfying thoughts from being present. Should a positive thought break through to the conscious mind, it is either immediately replaced by an unhappy one or the happy thought is reworked to give it a negative spin.

This type of thinking pattern is constantly lessening the chances the person has of feeling happy or building up self-esteem.

Some Main Points About Which the Family Should Be Aware

- The person cannot help it. It is recognized as part of the disorder.

- The process is so automatic it is given the name "automatic negative thinking" or ANT for short.

- The vast majority of the time, the negative recollections do not reflect events as they occurred.

- ANT is so powerful it can take an event and, by focussing in on and magnifying (or creating) negative events, the whole event is recalled as being generally negative. e.g., "I can't think of any happy times in our marriage. It has just been one big downer for me."

- Decision-making is very difficult for a person with anxiety/depression. Once a decision has been made the person will probably feel good about it—for a while. However, let ANT at it, and the points which now seem the strongest, are those which weigh against the decision which was made. "I screwed up again!" "I can't get anything right." "Why didn't I take the other choice?"

- The error in the thinking process is so strong, the person believes the negative spin to be true.

Examples

Tony sends a Christmas present to a friend. The friend does not reply. Tony immediately reaches the conclusion the present was so poorly selected it was not worthy of a response. In other words, it is Tony's fault.

Daphne passes a friend on the street and greets her. The friend does not reply. Daphne comes to the conclusion the friend is mad at her for some reason and tries to figure out what she has done wrong. Daphne is blaming herself. Actually, the friend didn't see her.

Stephen was sitting on the porch admiring his new car. It was just what he wanted. Other thoughts replaced the happy ones. "I paid too much." "Those tires look like they will puncture easily." "The antenna can be broken off easily." The spin-doctor is at work.

Carolyn has just retired from 25 years as an office manager. Her performance reports have been excellent. She can always think back on those years with a feeling of satisfaction. No she can't! Her automatic negative thinking ignores 99% of the good work she did and so strongly focuses in on the negative 1%, she has come to believe the 25 years were a disaster in which nothing went right. She has no positive memories for a very large portion of her life.

Marge loves shopping but her illness prevents her from getting out very often. Today she went shopping and her family did its best to see she had a good time. When they arrived back home Marge was feeling elated with her purchases and pleased to have been able to get out. She was tired and lay down for an hour. During that hour the spin-doctor in her head worked hard to turn the day into a negative event. When Marge woke up she was feeling down about the day. She was disappointed that she didn't get to a store she wanted to visit, unhappy with her purchases, blaming her family for not taking her to a certain restaurant. In short, she now "realized" she had had a miserable day. Her family was hurt and began to feel guilty for not having made Marge's day into what they had planned. Of course it was ANT at work but it affected the whole family.

Raquelle had worked for the same company for over 20 years. She was now on sick leave due to depression. Her pension was secure but she worried constantly it would not be enough once she began to collect it. The amount on the printouts she received showed it should be adequate but Raquelle worried constantly it had been miscalculated. Because of the circumstances the company rep came out to her house and worked it out by hand showing her how it was calculated. Satisfied, Raquelle felt better. Overnight ANT had been at work. When the rest of the family arose they found Raquelle working on the figures afraid there had been a mathematical error. Because it was mathematical it was fairly easy for a member of the family to sit down with her and check the figures. Feeling somewhat better Raquelle went on with her daily work. But only a few hours later she was back worrying. This time it was, "What if the inflation rate used in the calculations is wrong." The next morning it was something else she had thought might be wrong with the calculations…and so on.

Or it may be a matter of, "He said the returns would be 4%." (Actually he said historically the lowest the investment had ever returned was 4% but it was usually in the 10% range.)

How much time you want to spend going over individual items depends a great deal upon your patience and how strongly the person defends the thoughts which she *knows* are correct. Some people can be very defensive and upset if you tell them they are out to lunch on how they remember or perceive an event.

A program of cognitive behavioral therapy will give Raquelle tools she can use so that this constant problem finding/worrying does not occur.

Some other examples of turning happy thoughts into sad ones are:

Initial Thought	Replaced by Thought From the Past
I am enjoying this church dinner	I made a fool of myself by dropping a plate three years ago.
I did a good job pruning that tree	I once killed a broom bush by over pruning it.
That polished table looks great	Sand in my cloth once ruined a finish
I am going for a bike ride	Once put too much air in a tire and it blew up. Stupid me.
I like my new car.	I sure got taken on my first car. Idiot. I bet that salesman is still laughing at me.

The "Should Haves" and "If Onlys"

- A favorite tool of ANT is that of making the person feel they goofed.

- If only I had gone back and tried on that blue dress again.

- I should have said I wanted to go to Mayfair Mall. It would have turned out much better.

- I should have bought that blanket. Bet they are all sold now.

Blame here is placed both on herself and on her family. She really does believe she had a miserable day which could have much better if only they had done things differently.

Negative Thinking as a Protective Mechanism

Some professionals are now looking at negative thinking in a different light. In the case of those with some anxiety disorders they feel the negative thinking may be a "protective" strategy the brain has developed. Those with anxiety disorders are constantly on alert as they scan for threats. Positive thoughts can a make a person feel good and relaxed. Negative thoughts keep a person at a higher level of readiness as they remain uptight and worried.

Helping a Person Overcome Negative Thinking

One of the most effective methods is cognitive behavioral therapy (CBT). This can be done either by a professional or using one of the self-help books available on the topic. CBT is now offered over the Internet. Page 166 lists a site which offers it free.

One woman used a simple method to catch herself in the process of thinking negative thoughts. She stuck question marks around the house and whenever she saw one she would stop and monitor her thoughts

Main Points

• The person cannot help it.
• ANT is recognized as part of the disorder.
• The vast majority of the time, the negative recollections do not reflect the truth.

- ANT is so powerful it can take an event and, by focusing in on and magnifying (or creating) negative events, the whole event is recalled as being generally negative.
- The error in the thinking process is so strong, the person believes the negative spin to be true.
- The whole family can be trapped in the thinking process.
- The family may begin to feel guilty.
- The "should haves," "might haves," "if onlys," "what ifs," all play a powerful role in automatic negative thinking.

Eleven

Depression

DEPRESSION IS A SEPARATE DISORDER. It may exist on its own or in conjunction with other conditions. It is estimated 70% of those with an anxiety disorder will develop depression.

Remember that depression is a separate disorder. If a person with anxiety develops depression, then in addition to the anxiety symptoms, a person will also show those of depression.

The person suffering from it may not realize how far the depression has progressed. The constant feeling of hopelessness and despondency can sneak up so that the person does not even realize this is not the normal state of affairs and does not seek help. If left untreated it can eventually leave the person so mired down that she has little interest in getting up, eating or, even, continuing to live. Suicide may be the end product for some who have not been treated.

What Is Depression?

Like diabetes, depression is an illness. And, like diabetes, if not treated, it can be fatal. It can be fatal either through physical debilitation due to personal neglect or through suicide. It is not an illness to be treated lightly. The good news is that it is virtually 100% treatable.

We are all likely to have a few days of feeling down in the dumps but if this feeling of despair and sadness goes on for some time and/or has a negative effect on life style it is time for medical intervention.

Depression is the most commonly diagnosed mental disorder. Estimates suggest 15% of the population will develop depression to the degree it is serious enough to seek medical help. Serious depression is called "clinical depression."

Types of Depression

Bipolar Depression

This was originally known as manic-depression in which persons alternate between being depressed and being hyper or manic. In the manic phase they act as though they had been given too large a shot of energy. Going almost 24 hours a day, working at high speed, talking too fast, increased levels of high self-esteem, increase in libido (sex drive), etc.

Unipolar Depression

The person is always down, feeling depressed. This is the type of depression found in almost 100% of those who have developed it as a result of having an anxiety disorder.

Causes of Depression

Other than to say it is a disorder of the brain, involving certain chemical reactions, the exact cause is not fully understood. It is probably due to a combination of causes. These include:

Environmental Factors

This would include events such as job loss or severe problems at work, marriage breakdown, family stresses, financial problems, low self-esteem, and other negative events over which a person has little or no control (such as prolonged illnesses).

Personal Factors

The major item here is negative thinking in which a person focuses on the negative side of things rather than recognizing the brighter side. It is a constant case of, "My glass is half empty" vs. "My glass is half full."

Biological Factors

There are indications that the tendency for depression is genetic. Some physical problems can contribute to depression, such as an underactive thyroid. Other physical ailments include those which cause frequent pain, or make unwanted changes in a life style. Alcohol and some street drugs can also cause depression.

Why Does a Person with Anxiety Develop Depression?

At some time or other anyone with a prolonged anxiety disorder comes to feel she is not in control of her body. The panic attacks seem to come out of the blue and can severely limit her life style. The agoraphobia restricts her to her home or other bounded areas. There seems to be no end in sight. There may be financial problems that develop as a result of job loss with leads to more stress and feelings of guilt. Social life may have all but disappeared. Boredom mixed with constant fear. Negative thinking patterns, etc.

As you read this section keep in mind that recent research tends to indicate anxiety and depression are both caused by a similar chemical problem in the brain. Therefore, depression may not develop as a direct result of having anxiety, but as result of a similar chemical problem.

Symptoms of Depression

It is unlikely a person will show all of these symptoms. They are presented here for the sake of completeness. The symptoms and degree of severity can change almost from day to day.

Feelings:
• Loss of enjoyment from activities which used to be fun
• General feeling of low self-esteem, guilt, shame
• Feelings of sadness and despair
• Feeling empty
• A "Why should I bother?" feeling

It is not uncommon for the anxious person to develop depression as a result of months or years of not being able to control the source (her body) of the feelings which are producing the panic attacks, OCDs, negative internal talk or phobias. This is particularly understandable when you remember that the person suffering from any of these knows her actions are irrational but can do little about them.

Actions:
- General slow down of activities
- Body language is not positive, such as poor posture, just dragging around
- Withdrawal from friends and other social activities
- Excessive crying
- Insomnia
- Sleeping the day away
- Reduction or complete loss in sex drive
- Aches and pains with no discernible cause
- Loss of appetite
- Deterioration in dress, appearance and hygiene

Thinking Patterns:
- Negative thinking
- Feeling unworthy
- Thoughts of death, suicide or self-harm
- Poor memory
- Moderate to extreme difficulty making decisions
- Can't concentrate
- Difficulty making decisions.
- Can only work on thinking type projects for short periods of time

When I was at the depth of depression I had to have notes on the car seat telling me where I was going, what I was going for and, sometimes, even how to get there. When making a phone call I had to have a note in front of me to remind me what I wanted and whom I was phoning. In fact, I needed notes just to remember to prepare meals, get dressed, and for just about everything else. I even made one up with my wife's name on it just in case I forgot it. No, I didn't have to use that one.

What Can You Do to Help a Depressed Person?

That depends on the degree of severity. If the person is virtually noncommunicative there is not that much you can do other than ensure she eats and keeps up her personal hygiene as well as taking her medication. Talk to her, include her in conversations (whether she answers or not); encourage her to go out with you to a movie, a walk, shopping. Visit some understanding friends. Put on a TV program she likes. At this stage she really does need professional intervention but you can help while the medication is taking effect. Therefore, make certain you encourage her to obtain professional help if she is not already receiving it. And if she is receiving it, but there is no improvement, suggest she go back for more help. A change or adjustment of medication may be all that is required. Regardless of the degree of depression help her to arrange to get professional help.

Let the person talk. Listen to them and don't be judgmental. That is, don't keep saying things like, "That isn't true." "Nobody sees you that way."

Hugs, love and assurances go a long way.

Other Things You Can Do to Help

Have at least one thing planned for each day. This way she has something to get up for and to look forward to. It does not have to be something major—perhaps even working in the garden together or picking out a TV

show to watch that evening. Some people also get a lift
from cleaning out cupboards or doing other small jobs
with other people.

Where possible help the person to make decisions. I
have seen some people go over the same advertise-
ments for weeks as they try to make a decision about
purchasing a particular item.

Encourage her to keep in contact with her understanding friends. It could be just a short phone call but
any new social contact with uplifting people can help.

Going for walks in a park, smelling the flowers,
watching happy children at play can also help.

Where possible have a cheery room. Colors, pictures, favorite items, happy music can all help.

Make the person feel genuinely useful. In my case,
one factor that contributed to my depression, was the
feeling of uselessness. The rector at my church asked
me if I were capable of sorting out the congregation list
and putting it in a computer database. I wanted to but
didn't feel I had the energy. I was also somewhat in that
depressive fog depressed people understand well.
Nevertheless, I gave it a try. When I returned it to the
rector he gave me genuine praise and let it be known
amongst the congregation what I had done. For a short
period I almost felt on top of the world again. I wasn't
until a few years later I realized I had screwed up parts
of the list. He had never mentioned the mixed up parts.
He had managed to keep the conversation to the parts
I had done more or less well.

This rector played a significant role in my recovery
and I am grateful to him. Every Thursday morning after
Communion we would have coffee together and I was
able to talk to an understanding person.

My wife also played a major support role in my recovery. For several months she had to take on the entire running the house, reminding me to get dressed, shave, etc. At the same time she encouraged me to get out; make sure I had all my notes; remembered appointments for me and a dozen other things while all I did for several weeks was do nothing but play mindless games on my computer. Thanks, dear.

Suicide Talk

The Canadian Mental Health Association says it is all right to let the person talk of their feelings of suicide. Talking about it doesn't necessary mean she is planning to commit suicide. However, anyone seriously thinking about taking her life is in serious need of immediate professional help.

Another Aspect of Suicide

I am very pleased to see that one professional suicide prevention group has now begun to discuss an aspect of suicide which seemed to be almost taboo. I had received a few letters from people to whom this happened so it was not a surprise. I had just never seen it mentioned anywhere. Bruce's story is typical.

This is strange and frightening. It occurred just prior to me being diagnosed with depression. I was going through a particularly bad period with numerous problems both at home and at work.

I had been asked to pick up some groceries on the way home. As I drove out of the parking lot I got this idea in my head that I should kill myself on the way home. It seemed like the right and proper thing to do. I couldn't have really been thinking clearly on any level as I planned to drive up a mountain road, go over the side, then pick up the groceries and go home.

I was about 1/3 of the way up the mountain looking for a good place to drive over the edge when what I was doing suddenly hit me. I shook for almost a full day afterwards.

I wonder how many other people who suddenly jump, or drive off the road have been affected the same way? A lot of those who survive cry for help so perhaps they snapped out of it just a second or so too late.

Thanks, Bruce. I have received letters from others who have had similar experiences.

Other Resources

There are many good books and Internet sites available for depression.

Looking After Yourself

Don't allow yourself to be sucked down into her world of depression. It is very easy to allow it to happen.

Don't blame yourself or the family for her having depression. It is no more your faults than hers.

Understand there is no way she could "just snap out of it" at a moment's notice. She will improve but it will take time. Non-clinically depressed people can snap themselves out of it. Those with clinical depression usually cannot. Oh, they can work at it over time but don't expect an immediate shift.

Listening to a depressed person talk is more productive for the depressed person but don't let it go on all day.

Keep your own social life up. You are not ill and it is important that you remain well. Besides, just because one person is sick does not mean the whole family has to undergo a change of life style for the worst.

Have someone you can talk to about the situation. You must also be able to let off steam as well as get a reality check every so often.

To keep your friends, don't let depression dominate your topics of conversation.

Find some time for relaxing and learning methods of relaxation.

The person may begin to blame you for her condition. You are handy and she needs someone to take her frustration out on. Don't get in a fight over it. Gently walk away if necessary and then, when things are calmer, talk about it.

The same is true of being yelled at or otherwise put down. Just because she has a disorders does not give her the right to be rude or mean to you. On the other hand, don't have too thin a skin.

Try to avoid feelings of resentment on your part. Personal counseling may be necessary for you to keep the situation in perspective.

Main Points

- Clinical depression is a genuine serious medical problem
- Depression can be treated
- There are things you can do which tend to help a clinically depressed but don't feel guilty if you cannot do anything that helps. It is a disorder, which requires professional help.

Twelve

Getting Out

G ETTING OUTSIDE the house or off the property can be difficult for some people. Others have no problems if they stay in their own neighborhoods but have difficulty visiting places such as malls, stores, parks, etc.

In this chapter I have just covered getting out without having to be the automobile driver. Driving is covered in Chapter 13.

Leaving the House

As you have read elsewhere in this book, leaving a safe place can be very difficult, if not impossible, for some. For many this safe place is the house or the property. Several in our group have given suggestions they found useful. All are designed to desensitize the person to leaving a safe area . All the steps may not be necessary for some people and others may take longer to proceed from one step to the next. The points are suggestions

the caregiver may wish to make to the anxious person.
(If the person is receiving some other type of therapy,
it might be a good idea to check with the therapist
first.)

- Relax before going out of the house. Listen to calming music or whatever else works. Don't focus on
  going out and try not to fear it. It will not be necessary to proceed any further than you feel comfortable
  going.
- Sit on the doorstep and just watch the world or the
  wonders of nature.
- Perhaps have a purpose for leaving the house such as
  going to the gate for the mail.
- If you have a pet maybe walk a short distance with it.
  Sit with it on the doorstep or in the garden.
- Have someone with you if necessary. Maybe you just
  want to sit and talk for a while or maybe that is all
  you want to do today.
- If you are going for a walk up the block go with someone or have a person waiting for you some short distance away.
- Plan to meet someone at whatever distance away you
  feel comfortable. This person may be out of sight
  around a corner or be visible in the distance.
- If you feel more comfortable carrying a charm or
  teddy bear...why not?
- Taking a dog for a walk has helped several people.
- Listening to music during the outing has helped
  many. Make sure the music does not drown out any
  approaching traffic or you could end up squashed.
- Thinking about other things can help too.

- Crossing a road can be difficult. Have the person accompanying you cross it several times with you, then have the person wait on the other side for you. In time you will be able to cross the road and come back again with your support person waiting for you at the starting point.
- The busier the road the more difficult it seems to be. Stoplights can also give a trapped feeling as you have to wait for them before you can move.
- Don't be upset if one day you can't do what you did the day before. That is normal. Regaining this lost ground usually occurs much faster than it did the first time.

The above suggestions will probably not work in a straight line of improvement. Over some periods of time nothing may happen. At others, progress is made in baby steps and, from time to time, huge giant steps are taken.

There are a couple of stories I want to relate to you. I was out with a woman who could not walk along a certain section of busy road. We had driven about a mile away from her place and were just about to start walking when something happened and she became very mad at me. So mad in fact that she got out of the car and walked the mile back to her place along this busy road with no problems. Strange how it works.

The second story is about a woman who was finally able to walk to her community mail box but was terrified of having to stand there and open it. Actually, she had never been able to open it. One afternoon as she was standing there the postal delivery truck came by. She and the driver got into a brief conversation during which she explained her problem. The driver took about half an hour showing her all the parts of the box, putting letters into her box and letting her open it. It is nice to see there are those who will take time out of their schedule to help like this.

Stores and Malls

Oh, those stores and malls! Wide open spaces, enclosed spaces, crowding, noises, flashing lights, no nearby exits, getting caught in the flow, elevators, escalators, open staircases, overwhelming decisions...it is too much for many. The suggestions below were contributed by many people who found they helped. Again, it may have been baby steps, but they did work.

General Suggestions

Before getting specific suggestions, there are a few things to keep in mind.

- Don't blame yourself if the person has a panic attack or is unable to complete the outing. It's not your fault.

- Don't feel there is something you must be able to do to help the person get over a panic attack. There is little you can do. If at home the person may want to be alone or just held. If you are out, they may want to just sit for a few minutes or return home.

- The person you are with is in charge. They call the shots. If they want to abort the outing—abort. If they want to go somewhere other than where you planned—go there. That person knows what makes them feel most comfortable—you don't know.

- After a few outings try to have someone else come along. This way the person you are supporting will begin to feel comfortable with the other person. Eventually you don't have to be present all the time. Of course, it never hurts to have more than a couple of people ready to help out. During recovery, it may even be beneficial to have more people around.

- Don't wear yourself out. For your own health there may be times you have to say "no" to a request.

- You may not understand a panic attack but never tell the person it's all in her head or she could do it if she really wanted to. PAs and anxiety don't work that way.

- I prefer not to call outings "practices." Practices seems to give a sense of not expecting success. Since there is no specific goal, how can you have a failure? Every outing is a success if looked at correctly.

- As part of your support role you may have to remind the person that backsliding is normal, assure them they are sane and that they are not having a heart attack or other physical trauma.

- Do not be upset if you get snapped at occasionally. The person may be very up tight. That does not mean you have to be a wimpy doormat and take whatever is dished out to you. Just don't be too sensitive.

- Do not think these suggestions are rigid rules. They are not. Go with what comes naturally at the moment.

Specific Suggestions

Don't make a big deal of it. The person is probably anxious and to plan as though you were preparing an invasion will make them more anxious. How much preplanning, structure and preparation are required varies from person to person and will probably change over time.

- If you are not familiar with the place you plan to go, go ahead of time to case it out. See which areas will seem confined; find the exits, ask about times when it is not too crowded. Know where the stairs are located in case escalators or elevators are a problem. Being able to tell the person you know the area may make them feel less anxious.

- Try to find stairs rather than elevators or escalators. Sometimes I have had to ask the staff to open up a "staff only" stairway for us. And those open glass elevators...wow!

- If the person wants you to stay with them do so— like glue. It's not her job to keep her eye on you (but she usually does). It's your job to keep your eye on her.

- The person may want to hold your hand or she may suggest you stay a few feet back from her. Do what she requests.

- Always have an agreed upon central place picked out to meet in case you accidentally do become separated. Once it is obvious you have lost the person go directly to that spot. Do not waste more time looking. They will feel more comfortable if they know they can count on you to be there.

- If the person wants to leave you for a while, set a definite time and place where you will meet. Don't be late. It is better to be early in case the person has had to return early.

- The only responsibility I put on the person is to let me know if she is feeling overly anxious or panicky. It is frequently impossible to tell from just looking at them.

- If the person indicates they are becoming anxious ask them what they would like to do. Just take a few

deep breaths? sit down? go to a restaurant? leave the
building? return to the car? A break may be all that
is needed for her anxiety/panic level to lower. They
may wish to come home or return to the place they
left. That is up to them. Ask the question but don't
push.

- If they have an unmanageable panic attack lead them
from the area to a place where they feel safer. Don't
forget to see that they have no unpaid for items in
their hands. They probably wouldn't even be aware if
they did.

- Don't give the impression there is something you just
must buy before returning home—this adds stress.
Ask if it is OK to stop off somewhere but don't make
it sound mandatory.

- At all times be supportive but not condescending.

- Don't add to the anxiety by becoming frustrated or
losing your cool.

- Remember you are not responsible for her recovery.
You are doing what you can but the majority of the
healing must come from within.

- Going to the theater or a meeting can be a challenge. When the lights dim or the doors shut are the
hardest parts. Find a seat right at the exit and let
your partner know it is OK to leave. I usually found
most places were understanding and gave us a
refund.

- Going on the ferry to the mainland from Vancouver
Island was something we had to attempt many times.
The people in the ticket booth got to know me and
usually had a refund waiting when they saw we had
to drive out again.

Ingenuity works well, too
Creativity and imagination can all help. Here are some examples.

Ever thought of using a wheelchair for mastering places such as malls, ferry ramps, etc.?

Try putting the person you are looking after into a wheelchair and going around that way. I have had very good success with this. After one or two trips in a wheelchair it seems so much easier to get out of the chair part way through the outing and carry on. The support person will have the chair if it is needed.

I had never heard of the idea of a wheelchair being used. My 'discovery' of it was born out of desperation as I tried to help someone onto a ferry for an appointment with an anxiety professional. It did not look like it would be possible to have this person walk up the ramp onto the ferry and I was somewhat stymied until I saw the wheelchair sitting in the terminal. After a brief discussion, the person I was with said she would give it a try and away we went. I had also expected the six-deck ferry to be a problem but after a couple of rounds in the wheelchair she was up and away leaving me to baby-sit the chair.

Shortly after I mentioned the wheelchair as a tool for the support person, a support group in Venezuela told me they had been using walking canes for sometime. The canes allowed them to focus on something other than the surroundings and, if they felt dizzy, the cane helped to support them. Good idea.

Grocery carts also work well. Regardless of how dizzy or panicky she felt going up and down the aisles in stores, she just hung on to her grocery cart and didn't look out of place at all. Ah, but stopping to make a decision on food items—yes, well, that took a bit longer but we made it.

Other Situations

The anxious person may need you when they go into doctors' or dentists' offices. Understanding medical people usually don't object, especially when they realize they may have to deal with a panic attack if you aren't there. A sense of humour helps in unusual situations and you may be able to joke them along. Other times they may feel more comfortable by just telling you to shut up.

Some of the things I have done are:

- Making certain we took the right cassettes to the dentist for the person to listen to while having work done
- Suggesting to the dentist a rubber dam may not be the best idea nor is using adrenaline in the anesthetic
- Holding hands while they were in the dentist's chair
- Making certain everything being done to them during tests and other medical procedures is explained to them both before the test and as it is being done
- Holding hands while they were having a biopsy under a local anesthetic
- Discreetly looking the other way while holding a hand during an EKG (heart test).
- Climbing inside a CAT scanner so I could describe the tunnel to them before they were moved in
- Sitting in post-op so they had a familiar face to wake up to
- Making phone calls for them if the situation may be stressful.

You never know what is next.

We All Goof

Being human we are not perfect. Every so often we make a mistake. One of my major ones was on a shopping trip with a lady. It was to be the first time she tried shopping on her own with me meeting her at various locations. In case something happened and we missed each other, our final fall back position was the car. Somehow we missed each other. After a few minutes of looking I headed out to the car. The problem was I had forgotten where I had parked the car. I just couldn't find it. To anyone who could have seen both sides it probably looked like a Laurel and Hardy comedy. The woman had the mall page me three times and each of the three times was when I had gone outside again to try to find the car. On the fourth try, the page and I connected and I found this very distraught lady waiting at a door of the mall, which was adjacent to the area I had parked the car.

Airline Trips

Airline trips can be very stressful to some with anxiety disorders. A couple of years ago I was helping a women prepare for a plane trip to visit her family. The staff of WestJet Airlines Ltd. here in Victoria, B.C. was very helpful. They went out of their way to see everything possible was done for this potential passenger.

I phoned ahead to explain the problem Dana would have in the airport. Without any hesitation we were invited to come to the airport. When we arrived a very compassionate young man obtained a Visitor's Pass for her and spent over an hour taking her through the airport. He explained what would occur and allowed her to make several trips through security and the halls to the gates until she felt comfortable. The staff was great and I am thankful there are companies which will go out of their way to accommodate those with anxiety disorders.

Regrettably it seems as though this help may be almost a thing of the past. WestJet has recently informed me that although they would like to continue this special help, the increased security, government regulations, and busy flight schedules have made it increasingly difficult. However, WestJet will still attempt to accommodate people with special requests such as these whenever possible. I do hope the same consideration is given by other airlines.

Thirteen

Driving

PEOPLE SUBJECT TO PANIC ATTACKS can find driving difficult. It is frequently one of the last problems to be
overcome as they make progress in their recovery. The
usual reason given is that the person is afraid of a panic
attack while driving. This is true but the more immediate fear is that they will encounter some situation
which triggers a panic attack.

There are some people who find their car a safe
place but they seem to be in the minority.

Triggers of Panic Attacks

When anyone first starts driving it seems as though
there are a hundred things that must all done at the
same time. Watch the traffic; watch the road; watch for
stoplights; don't hit that pothole; go back and apologize
to that nice motorcycle policeman you just forced into
the ditch; use the breaks; change gears; find the wiper

switch—oops that was the hood release. And on top of all that you have to learn to ignore the thousands of other unimportant pieces of data which are flooding your brain. Most of us did it successfully. Remember that a person with high anxiety is hyper-vigilant. In the case of driving it means much of the unnecessary data registered by the senses is not filtered out but is sent on to the higher thinking parts of the brain to be processed, identified and evaluated. Rather than the brain just concentrating on information needed to drive safely, it attempts to register and process things which are immaterial to driving. The result is a sensory overload worse than you may find in hard rock videos.

Sounds can be enough to trigger a panic attack—the whooshing of traffic in other lanes, horns and the sound of tires from many vehicles on the highway.

Visual stimuli are also a villain. Many cars going in different directions, headlights from moving vehicles, the flashing by of utility poles, white lines which are not clearly visible, the multitude of road signs and direction signs, all play a role.

A while ago I was talking with a two women who were having trouble driving. One was a musician, the other an artist. The musician was troubled primarily by the noises while the artist was having her greatest problem with the overload of visual information. Makes sense.

Not being in control of the situation is another trigger. Being forced into the wrong lane, not being able to change lanes when required, missing a turn, becoming lost, being tapped at a stoplight, being forced to take an unfamiliar route, or not being able to follow the planned route, all raise the level of anxiety to the point a panic attack may occur.

Getting Started Driving Again

There are a number of ways a person can start driving again. Here are some which have been successfully used. Not all work for everyone and a combination may be the best way. Whichever method you are going to help the person utilize, remember not to push too much. They do not need a support person raising their anxiety level beyond a small touch. Also, be aware that it can be very disheartening for someone to have to fight in order to drive over a familiar stretch of road that they have been driving over for years without a second thought.

Don't let the person feel like a failure because a particular method is not working for her. I hear of very few people who find an instantaneous cure. It takes times and practice. Practice by using the baby steps we talked about in an earlier chapter. Even taking a break for a few days may be preferable if a high level of anxiety is being reached. Make sure that short break does not turn into a long time.

Remember to include a bit humor if possible and if it is welcomed. Some people find the humor helpful, others don't. Also, give genuine praise where it is due. Even a very small step, like having the willpower to try, is worthy of praise. But don't be surprised if the person responds with something like, "So what? I was doing that for years." Such can be the life of a support person.

Methods

These don't have to be done in any particular order or in any time frame. Let the person be the guide. On the other hand, the person may feel better if someone takes charge and lays it out. That is something you will have to work out with the anxious person.

The first step could be to have the person feel comfortable in the car. Maybe just sitting in it herself for a while, then starting it up, moving a bit in the driveway or in a deserted parking lot, are all methods of desensitization.

Take her for a ride along a quiet familiar route. She is going to be worried about becoming trapped and having a panic attack, so look for places on the road where she can pull off and not feel threatened. Also, find places where she can turn around if she feels she has gone far enough.

Next, let her drive the section with you sitting beside her. Just having you there can give her confidence in knowing she will not be stuck if she can't continue. Without the fear of any help being available during a possible panic attack, she may be able to do the whole route on her own—with just a few anxious moments.

Perhaps follow along behind her in a second car. Keep up with her and don't drop back out of sight. Just the knowledge that help is available may be enough to see her through.

Use a cell phone if you have one. Staying back out of sight or remaining at home but available at the push of a button will also give some confidence. Preprogram one button on her phone to call home. During a panic attack she may forget the number or how to dial it. Oh, yes, and stay off the line...she doesn't need to find her lifeline busy.

Suggestions for Driving on Her Own

The cell phone option I have already mentioned. Other

things that have been successfully tried are given below. Again, remember, they may take time and not all will be useful to each individual.

- Place some stuffed toy such as a teddy bear on the passenger seat.
- Play quiet relaxing music in the car.
- Listen to the 'little girl inside" as she says it is OK to stop now, OK to go on.
- If sound bothers her, suggest closing the window and sunroof.
- Sneak up on stoplights. Crawling slowly towards them ensures the car will not to come to a complete halt before the green light. This way she does not feel trapped or stuck.
- Use a road map to plan a route that avoids trouble spots such as left hand turns, center lanes, overpasses, under-passes, tunnels, multi-lane highways, etc. This will prevent a trapped feeling, caused by being stopped on an inside lane and avoids the overpowering visual signals from high sides such as under-passes and bridges.
- Perhaps three people with trouble driving may wish to go together. With three in the car there is, maybe, not so great a chance of an uncontrollable panic attack occurring. Or, when comfortable, these people may all wish to drive together in separate cars.
- A novel idea was used with mixed success by a group of people who had no one to drive with them. They had met over the Internet and decided they would each go for a drive at exactly the same time and pretend they were together. It worked for two of the three of them.

- Prior to a drive, visualizing the route has worked for some. This is rather similar to an athlete at a sports event before doing it.
- If she does have problems suggest she pull over and wait the panic attack out. For several reasons it is possibly better to wait it out rather than trying to continue to drive. On the other hand, if the anxiety level is not too high, the person may want to continue on without pulling over. This is a judgment call.
- Ensure there is enough gas in the car and a road map in case a wrong turn is made.
- Where possible going from one safe place to another is helpful. For instance going from the house to a friend's place seems to help.
- Having the support person wait at a particular location also seems to help.

Other Points

It takes longer for some than for others to be able to drive virtually panic free. For some it is weeks. For others it is much longer but, as with all progress, each baby step is victory.

A "new" car can cause some backsliding or, at least, a higher level of discomfort. The car feels different, plus the controls and switches are in different places.

It may take awhile to conquer a particular stretch of road. One woman I was working with took over a year to be able to drive the last 1/4 mile (.4 km) through a park because this section had no place to pull over. She could do both ends of this section but not the middle. Rather than just keep pounding her head against a wall she took other routes and returned to this one from time to time.

As with other situations, there will probably be back-sliding. This is normal and the lost ground will usually be recovered quickly.

Here is an example of a woman who did not give up despite events which would have upset a lot of us. She wanted to drive down a particular five mile stretch of road. After several days she felt she was ready to do it on her own. I remained at her house in case she had to use her cell phone. If she did phone I would talk her through her attack, remind her of her relaxation techniques, etc. I was really hoping I did not have to go get her.

The first evening she went on her own I received a phone call, "Come and get me. I have just hit a dog." Ouch! She didn't need that and she was so upset I did go down to escort her back. The second evening she was ready to try again. "Come and get me. I have just run over a chicken." I talked her down from that one and she returned home a bit shaken. On the third evening she was full of confidence. "Come and get me. I have just hit a deer". I went to get her and to ensure she and her car were unhurt. She was shaken up but OK and somewhat nervous about doing the route again.

At this point I thought it might help if I followed her and if she drove it in the opposite direction. It was starting to grow dark when I saw her car weaving over both sides of the road. As I got closer I saw about 8 deer running across the road in front of her and behind her. GADS! Next time we will not use this road, we'll use another road instead. The next evening she started off in the direction she had decided on. She was relieved that she would not have to worry about dogs, chickens or deer. Then I heard on the phone, "Come and get me. I have just hit another deer and it is down on the road."

I really have to give her an "A" for persevering. After that week of disasters she no longer seemed like a scared rabbit, but it was certainly a stressful week.

Giving Yourself Permission

Below is a letter from a woman who responded to my request for stories about learning to drive again. It contains many of the points we discussed above.

A letter from Anne

Dear Ken,

After a number of years of not being able to drive (I really had tried), I came up with an approach which worked for me.

Basically, it was a change in my thinking. The thought process is—I'm going out, I'm going to have fun, I'm not setting myself goals, I'm going to do what I want to do and check with myself as to what I can, want or not want to do.

Why did I try this? First, because I had had enough failures—I didn't want more and I was not going to set myself up for them anymore. Second, the joy and fun had gone from life. Third, I was tired of being dependent on others. Fourth, I was worn out from panic attacks.

To drive was my big thing so at first I just drove around a small area near the house. If I became uncomfortable, I'd pull over and ask not why I was uncomfortable but if I should do more, go home or go somewhere else. I listened to the little voice inside (was it me or the inner child—I don't know), but I quickly found the voice was correct. If it was me then I was simply telling myself—yes, go on; no, go somewhere else; try another road; time to go home. I even got lost a few times which previously was a guarantee of an attack, but now it wasn't—I found new places instead. This checking with myself was in essence giving myself permission to do what I wanted to do. It gave me choices and gave me back some control.

What if I panicked? If I felt it coming or it came, I went home. Avoidance—yes. But it usually only happened when I didn't listen to or check with myself. After all those years, I was driving—going to appointments, the bank, shopping centers and malls and able to buy things on my own. I even found myself going over overpasses and "managing" left hand lanes. I guess it was a lightening up, not taking driving so seriously and letting recovery happen at its own pace. It happened relatively quickly and with a minimum of panic and, in addition to driving, it is spreading into other areas of my life. Do I still have panic attacks? Yes, but rarely when I am driving.

This approach has helped another person with agoraphobia and I hope it is useful to others. It is not a 100% answer to everything; I'm still on medications, but it got me out of the house. I felt like framing the first gas bill I got in years.

Anne

Anne had come to realize her previous thinking process was setting her up for failure and she made changes.

There is a world of difference between "I am going for a drive" and "I am going to try to go to the store. " In the first, the aim is to go for a drive. It may be to the end of the block or 12 blocks and back. Anne did what she felt comfortable doing. In the second case, Anne would have had to make it to the store or she would have failed to achieve her goal.

The same is true of any event whether it be a walk off the property or a drive. Why make a big thing out of trying to drive to the store when she can have a much more relaxed attitude just going for a drive and doing whatever she feels comfortable doing? Turn right. Turn left. Come home. Keep going. It doesn't matter. Allowing herself to have a freedom of choice without feeling guilty or under pressure is, to her, the key.

After a few weeks of this Anne found she was driving greater distances and, eventually, could set off for a specific location knowing she had been there before while on her "no pressure" drives. She can now drive virtually anywhere. Stoplights and inner lanes are still a bit of a problem but not enough to force her to use alternate routes.

Main Points

- Driving is one of the more difficult tasks to relearn.
- Hypervigilance causes the brain to become overloaded.
- The overload and stress can lead to panic attacks.
- Many find it helpful to pick out a non-stressful route.
- There are several ways of keeping stress to a minimum while driving.

- Taking a "no failure" attitude and accepting baby steps as a positive achievement is key for many people as they relearn to drive without their anxiety level soaring.

Fourteen

What is it Like to be a Support Person?

THE ROLE OF A SUPPORT PERSON is not a bed of roses. It can be tiring, frustrating, confusing and very time-consuming.

In this chapter I have concentrated on those giving support to people with panic attacks and agoraphobia but the general principles are similar for most types of anxiety disorders and the specifics for the other disorders are covered in more detail elsewhere in this book.

Most of those who are primary support people are members of the family—usually the spouse. Unless the support person is prepared for the role it can be years of hell. Properly informed for the role, it can be a time in which both support person and the person with anxiety can grow.

Not too long ago Paula contacted me on the Internet looking for information and contacts with others who were support people. Her letter illustrates many of the problems a person just thrown into the role of support giver can encounter.

A Letter From Paula:

Ken, feel free to use this. If I can be of help to anyone, it will be great...there have been plenty of times I've felt like I was the only person in the world feeling these feelings, and then I felt guilty because I was thinking of myself and not Dave. If I can help one person, it will mean all the things I've been through haven't been in vain...

How do I cope...hmmm...well, for a while my "method" of coping was grouching and yelling at him and getting it off my chest, till I found out it made him worse, then I almost felt like I ended up in the nuthouse trying to keep in all the feelings and such. Now I just vent my feelings at my mother and she listens and then lectures...it works better, for sure. My biggest problem has been my anger and resentment because I've basically had to give up my entire life to cater to him; drive him to and from work because he can't drive as of yet, drive him to doctor's appointments etc, and basically hold his hand any time he's outside the house. I've never thought myself a strong person till this came up; now he relies on me for all the support, while I have to hold myself up. It's hard at times. I had to give up a good job because it wasn't flexible enough to work around driving him.

Ah, well....things are looking better lately. He has gotten better with driving and is trying to overcome the problems. Now he is on medication our marriage has settled down to a dull roar also ...he isn't a bear anymore!

I have found a few pen pals with the same problems my husband has so this has helped me quite a bit. It is much better to hear from another what he is going through...makes it easier to understand. I'm much too close to him, and he is also not very good at explaining it.

Paula

Paula's letter strongly illustrated why I worked with Steve Ward setting up the tAPir grassroots anxiety page on the Internet in 1995. The support people I came into contact with looked like lost confused individuals who did not seem to understand the disorder, did not know their role, nor where they were going. Like Paula, most support persons find themselves in a frustrating situation for which they are unprepared and ill-informed. Until recently the help available to the sick person did not seem to extend to include the support person. But, now that there is more information available, compare Paula's letter to Shelaugh's.

Dear Ken,

When my boyfriend and I first started to date we went everywhere together. Then after the 09-11-01 attacks he was not able to do as much as we first did. Then he got to the point that he was unable to leave the house at all.

My first reaction was to get mad. Here I was turning my life upside down for him and he did not seem appreciative. But I decided to learn about panic and anxiety before I made the decision to leave him. Boy, am I glad I did.

Yes, our lives as a couple are based on what he is able to do. We rarely plan anything and if we do go out it is to places he feels comfortable. There are still days where I feel like I don't get a say in what we do. But I am not the one that lives in fear 24 hours a day, 7 days a week. He tries his hardest to make sure that when I have something that needs to get done that we get it down. For example I just bought a new computer with his help, we went to several different stores and on two different nights. We did have to leave one store, but only one store, that is an accomplishment. As an individual I can still go out and do the things I like.

We have grown so much closer since we decided to work things out. One thing that I have noticed through all of this is that if I don't get upset with him, when we have to leave a store, turn the car around, or when we can't even go out at all, is that he is able to do more. He doesn't seem to get as anxious because he knows that if he is unable to do something I will not be upset.

Quite a difference. And it is encouraging to see there are now groups which work together to make this help for anxiety caregivers widely available.

This last letter shows the responsibilities which can be laid on others including that of 'a family secret.'

Mr. Strong,

I first want to thank you for your efforts to build a support structure for the support people. It is comforting to know there are others who are going through the same situation as you are. Thanks.

First I should let you know I am battling the feelings of betraying her trust. We don't talk about her illness outside of the house. I know in my mind that I am doing the right thing to seek out an answer but somehow I feel that I should just grin and bear it. This is very hard to do.

My wife has been suffering from panic attacks for the past 11 years. This has progressed from panic attacks to agoraphobia. Additionally, she has developed OCD always washing her hands. Each washing session take about 10 minutes. She has her safe zones for driving to school to pick up our daughter but is unable to shop or run errands alone. Consequently she is drawing our daughter into the safe person role. (I just read an article whereby the difference was explained). I am unable to spend as much time in this role due to my work schedule and commitments. I am wanting to relieve my daughter from this position to allow her to be a teenager.

I want to voice my feelings about this whole situation but am afraid the facts about the pressure this situation is placing on the family will be too much for her to handle. We recently had a discussion about her behavior but she took it very personally and does not want to see the effects this is having on our marriage. This is getting very frustrating and I am really losing interest in her as a person. I feel I am taking care of another child and am having to do it alone. My question is, are these types of feelings normal? I want to make this marriage work but it is getting very very difficult. I am finding myself desiring a more normal relationship whereby I can share with someone who can respond emotionally.

I also want to add that her emotional problems, I believe, extend from her abusive childhood whereby she was verbally abused and sexually abused by a parent. I have tried to get her to go to therapy but she refused after getting very angry and expressing this anger.

If you could provide any recommendations as to what I should do I would be most appreciative.

Kindest Regards

My reply with four questions and his reply with the answers:

I have four questions before I begin to answer you.

Q. Does your wife's therapist know of these problems?

A. She is not seeing a therapist. She believes that she will just have to deal with this the rest of her life. She is sort of giving up and saying that this is as good as it will get. She has made progress from when things first started. She used to not be able to drive even with someone in the car. Now she can drive but she and I would like her to do more. She still cannot take a walk and constantly needs an escort to go the simplest of places (mall, grocery store, etc.)

Q. What is your wife's therapist doing about it? Is she having any Cognitive Behavior Therapy or just medications?

A. No professional treatment or medications. She has read books but these do not seem to have done any good. I believe that this is bigger than a person can conquer while looking from the inside out.

Q. Do you mind if I strip your identification off of it and send it out to our group for comment? I will forward the answers to you and maybe, when you feel more comfortable, you would like to join the group. I think this will be a great help as you will likely receive responses from both caregivers and those with the disorders. Our group is composed of both professionals and non-professionals and I am sure you will receive some useful input.

A. Go ahead.

Q. How is your daughter responding to this?

A. There are periods of resentment between them at times. As of right now things have settled down, however, as patience ebbs tempers will flare.

I am thinking of sitting down with her to try to explain what Mom is going through. Again the betrayal feelings come into play. As of now, as work demands are letting up, for the time being, I plan to take up some of the escorting duties on the weekend.

Other chapters in this book contain information in detail for the support person but here is an overview upon which to build.

Throughout this book there are many suggestions on how to go about handling various situations. The points which follow are general in nature but form a platform from which the specific situational recommendations follow.

How should I adapt during the recovery process? Recovery is a process. It may take a short time or require a longer period. During the recovery every little step should be noted and genuine congratulations given. The person may or may not be excited about it. They may just think, "So what? I used to do that all the time." Try to change that thinking but it is the anxious person who must pat herself on the back and recognize a genuine step. Over a three-year period I spent many summer days on a wharf watching a small ferry sail away without us because the woman I was with could not get on it—or if she did—we had to get off again. Finally we were able to take the ride and I thought she would be delighted. No, she looked back on the time she had lost because she could not go for the short ride. Disappointing for me but it is all part of the role.

Try to change the thinking processes from "What ifs" to "So whats". And the "Shoulds" to "I will do it when I choose to". The first gets the person out of the "worrying about consequences" and the second removes the urgency and pressure that they seem to bring on themselves quite a bit. As one author put it, "Don't should on yourself."

Do a reality check on yourself every so often. It is very easy to be dragged into the person's way of thinking and reacting if you are not careful.

Don't push yourself on the person as they begin to need you to a lesser degree. It is sometimes difficult to recognize that you are not needed as much. Even when you do recognize it, you will probably still feel as though you are on guard and have trouble getting down from that level of vigilance. Certainly don't feel you are being pushed aside. This is what you have been working for all along—to bring the person back to a level of being able to function more on her own. It will probably seem like a hole in your life. Fill that hole with other activities but let the person know you will be there she needs you and be sure to make the person know you share in her happiness.

Some support people do have a difficult time letting go of the role. These people should check what the reasons are. They may have needs not previously recognized. There are other ways of meeting these needs depending upon what they are. If a person really does have a need to be required, he or she might try offering their services to a volunteer agency to get people out, etc.

What do I do during setbacks? Setbacks are an expected part of the healing process. It is like learning a new sport. The sick person will make progress then may reach a plateau during which no improvement seems to occur or, they may even slide back. Again, don't blame yourself. The person will probably be discouraged; remind her it is normal and they will most probably make rapid strides as she regains the lost ground. Remind them how far they have come. She may not be in a mood to listen but try it. You *may* want to discuss with her any changes which have occurred in her life or eating habits which could have brought this slide about. You may find nothing you can identify—don't expect an answer for every up and down.

What if the person does not want to get better? This is difficult because you are not in a position to judge whether she is trying or not. You should talk it over with a professional but, after you are sure, there is not much you can do other than withdraw support. There may be reasons why the person does not want to get better. She may be afraid of returning to the world from which she has "escaped". She may be a person who craves the attention shown to her Whatever the cause there is no reason you should devote your life to this behavior. Don't just withdraw it cold and don't feel guilty. Talk it over with the person then, trying to ignore the tears and possible guilt trips, make alternative arrangements to see that she is not left on their own. Church groups, volunteer drivers, close friends or relatives may be called upon to offer minimal support where needed. Where more intensive support is needed, see a local mental health agency or doctor. They may be able to recommend a group home or respite center.

What if I can't be a support person or I can't carry on? It is no shame to be unable to take on the role. Some people just are not made for it. If you can't, explain to the person it is nothing personal but you just can't do it or cannot carry on. Don't let your health suffer. If the person has no one else to turn to, contact some of the groups mentioned above.

The support person who can't carry on may wish to obtain counselling so there will be no feelings of guilt lingering in her mind.

1. Understand the illness. You do not have to be an expert in the illness but at least learn enough to know the symptoms and, generally, what is going on inside the person.

2. Once a competent diagnosis has been obtained, accept it and move on from there.

3. Don't assume you know what is best for the person with anxiety. Ask her. She usually has a fair idea. Also, listen to what the person is telling you. She will tell you what she is comfortable doing and how she would like you to act.

4. Don't be impatient. Healing can take time.

5. When necessary assure her she is not insane and that she will get better. Don't make it hollow; anxious people are very sensitive to honesty and insincerity.

6. Be predictable. They don't like fast changes to plans or surprises.

7. If you are at a business meeting with the anxious person don't butt in unless asked to but do keep your eyes open for her beginning to fade. After some time these people may become very tired and just agree to almost anything proposed. Sometimes they are not even aware this is happening.

8. Within reason, don't stop the ill person from talking about the disorder or negate what they say about the way they feel.

9. If you are at a medical appointment with the person and her answers do not seem to be forthcoming, find out why. Maybe she does not feel comfortable answering them, she has forgotten the answer, or she has just faded out. I find it very helpful for the two of us to make up a list of symptoms and questions ahead of the appointment and check each off as it is covered.

10. Do not feel guilty if the person has a panic attack or does not seem to be getting better. It is not your fault. You can only supply support; the healing must come from within.

11. During a panic attack the person may feel the need for reassurance that they not going to die. Hugs, etc. Or maybe they just want to be left alone. Ask them.

12. Don't let the person down by making promises you cannot keep. Many people with anxiety illnesses have grown up in an atmosphere of broken promises and disappointments.

13. It is helpful if all members of the family can sit down and talk together about the anxiety disorder, as well as sharing knowledge and ideas.

14. Be sure you and the ill person are very clear on what information about her illness will be given out and to whom. If the person does not want information given out then see if they would be comfortable with you just saying they have a chemical imbalance. Again, don't let them down. They have trusted you. However, I have found friends react better if they know the cause of the problem and not just assume you have faded from sight for some unknown reason. If you do decide not to tell anyone, be sure the reason is not shame. There is no need for shame at all.

15. If you do decide not to tell anyone make certain there is one exception. You need some trusted person with whom you can talk.

16. Don't allow the person to use so much avoidance she sits on her butt all day. Don't accept she can't do anything. If you both believe she can't, little progress will be made.

17. When something goes wrong try not to let her anxiety level make yours go up. For instance—Your garage door needs repairing. If five minutes after the repair person has left, the door comes off the tracks, she may be more upset than the situation calls for. Make certain you are calm before placing the necessary call to have the door put back on its

tracks. It is sometimes easy to begin to reflect another person's anxiety.

18. The same reflection applies to any minor crisis or problem, which comes up. She may look at all crises and problems as major ones. Weigh each problem out and act accordingly.

19. Laughter is a great healer. Benny Hill and Mr. Bean videos are very popular in anxiety and depression support groups.

20. Make sure nobody in the family is feeling guilty about the person having the disorder. More and more evidence is pointing to it being biochemical in nature just like an under-productive thyroid is a biochemical problem.

21. Keep up as many social contacts as you can for the whole family including the anxious person.

22. Try to make the home a supportive environment.

23. Even the smallest positive step deserves to be congratulated. But make sure it is sincere praise.

24. Set the ground rules together with the person you are supporting. You are there as a support person not as a butler or a maid. Say what you are capable of doing and see what you can work out with the sufferer. Unless they are temporarily confined to bed with frequent severe panic attacks and/or agoraphobia, they can still do some housework, typing, etc. Since you are giving up your time to help them, they should, if at all possible, be willing to pick up some of your work or chores. Remember, though, that panic attacks can leave a person very tired. If they are tired one day they may be able to do the work the next or the next.

25. Have someone you can go to. You must let off steam and be able to talk—friends, clergy, counselors, your doctor.

26. It is natural to feel sad or mad or frustrated about the disorder. Again, have someone you can talk to about it.

27. Make time for yourself. Don't let your entire life revolve around the illness. You are not ill and, for your own health, you must carry on as normal a life as possible. Have other people available who will be willing to help with the driving, taking the person shopping, phoning them, dropping in, etc. Remember you cannot be on call 24 hours a day. Your health won't take it. Church groups and mental health groups and volunteer agencies including volunteer drivers may all be able to help out.

28. Find ways to get out. Don't let your friends and social contacts go by the wayside. It happens too easily. Don't let two lives suffer.

29. Retreats, mini-vacations and respite centers all offer something to the support person who needs a break.

30. Don't let the anxiety disorder always be the main topic of conversation in the house. Life still goes on and it is much better if you are not sitting it out.

31. Do not quit your job. The person with anxiety may be afraid of being alone. As she reacts to an immediate need, the support person is frequently begged to leave a job to stay home with her. Leaving the job can cause financial hardships and, later, resentment at having given up a good job or career path. Besides, you, as a support person, have your own life to live as well.

Fifteen

A Cry from the Heart

IRECEIVED THIS LETTER FROM a support person last spring and eventually posted it (with permission) on a professional anxiety news list on the Internet. Because of the intense nature of the letter I had no intention of posting it on our own anxiety news list. I felt many may be upset by it and some fail to recognize it was an extreme case. I was wrong! I eventually had to post it. It was so full of mental anguish I called it "A Cry From the Heart." It was very well received. Several wrote to me saying how much it relieved their minds to know their experiences were not isolated. I have included one representative response which is on page 169.

P.S. This support person has now received the support as well as the professional help he needed and is much better.

Dear Ken;

It's 5:45 am. There is a whimpering coming from the person beside you and the bed is shaking. She is having another panic attack—the third tonight. She has tried hard to be still and not wake you but now she knows you are awake. Her arms go around you and the whimpers become full sobs. You hold her tight and tell her it is all all right. Everything will settle down in a few minutes. One part of you is trying to get back to sleep while the other is staying awake because you know that to her the bed is rolling, the walls falling inward, her heart is pounding and her hands feel like they are swelling up to the size of beach balls.

Today is your day off which means she will be able to come out of the bedroom and be with you. Since the agoraphobia set in she has not been able to leave the bedroom unless you are home. She has awakened some time ago but is afraid to tell her body it is time to get up and cause that initial surge of adrenaline, as it will bring on another attack. Because it is a special day with you home she does get up then slowly, hanging on the railing, makes her way into the kitchen. She walks like a drunkard but you know that is because her legs are rubber, the floor is seething and the lights overhead seem to be falling on her.

The next day is a work day. About 11 am comes a phone call from her crying for help. She has been fighting an attack since 9 am but can't seem to remember her exercises to bring herself back down. The secretary is very good at putting her calls through immediately. You excuse yourself from the group and take the phone to take on the process of bringing her down. You are worn out from it but your voice, somehow, assumes a calm tone and you gently tell her what to do. It was so much easier when there were other people to help but friends gradually drifted away due to the frequent last minute broken engagements, a fear of mental illness (which this is not) and the relatives have all found reasons not to be involved. Who else does she have? No one.

You arrive home much earlier than usual. In the bedroom she is sitting on the bed and trying to hide the bottle of narcotics she has been staring at for some time. You gently take the bottle, kiss away her tears of shame and tell her it is all right, you love her just as much as when you were first married and will always be with her. You talk about the time she will be better...and hope there will be one. Everyone does get over it eventually —so you are told. You fully understand why the divorce rate is over 80%—but the echo of "in sickness and in health" keeps running around in your head. And the suicidal thoughts do not surprise you as she still has all her mental faculties but she can't control what is going on inside her body—a great recipe for depression. The suicide rate is extremely high. Sometimes you walk in the door not knowing if you will find a living person or a body—maybe she was asleep when you phoned or just didn't hear it, or maybe...

It's November and she has her heart set on buying you a Christmas present all by herself. There is no hope of it being a surprise as you have to stay within a few feet of her at all times or the waves of a panic attack start flowing in her. Several times she tries to go into the store but you end up back at her safe place in the car. Finally she makes it into the store, grabs almost the first thing she sees and pretends you are not with her. Come Christmas Day you will both act as if you had no idea of what you were getting. But that will be Christmas Day. In the immediate future you know she will sleep most of the next few days from the energy exerted in doing the best she could for you.

The time has come for her to try to start driving again. Hopefully this will take some of the pressure off you. You have both spent weeks going out together with her driving sometimes and you driving when she found she could not continue. She has a cellular phone. You can stay at home and relax. Not likely, you have to sit by the phone to ensure the line is free if she needs it. You are just as much on watch as if you were with her. When she does phone you have to gently talk her back to the house or to one of the "safe places" she has identified so she can wait until you can reach her.

It has been a good week. No panic attacks and the agoraphobia seems to be lessening. She can get out a bit by herself. She is even starting to be able to make *some* decisions again. Unfortunately the lack of control she had with the panic attacks has left her with little to no confidence in the decisions she has made. They are constantly being re-examined and there is a fear there which makes it almost impossible to take a definite step. On top of this she has become so fear driven that every small event is catastrophized. Do you leave her to work it out herself or again assume that calm voice and talk rationally to her about it? God—we have come to assume a frightened child/parent relationship. Where is the person I married? Where is the relief for you? You don't even have the sex to help remove the tension as the last thing a depressed person is thinking of is sex. Also, who wants sex when the adrenalin flow will bring on another panic attack? That part of your life was denied you years ago.

You know there is a build up in tension in her because she is starting to yell at you again and taking everything the wrong way. Dealing with her is like walking on eggs. You are almost wishing for her to have an attack to get it over with. She will sleep for some time afterwards which is the only peace you get.

Calgary, Alberta
Dear Ken;

Thank-you for posting this. The story comes as no surprise as my husband and I have gone through it, though a little less extreme. The tears are running down my face, as I think what has been going on in my wonderful husband's mind. I thank GOD daily for your book, as it has given us the strength to keep working at our marriage. Now that my depression has lifted, I think that if I had not become ill with depression, and panic disorder, I wouldn't have met all my good friends—Ken you are one, and become a fuller, more compassionate person. It has also done this for my husband who before living with me, wouldn't have understood or cared about people with our disorder.

Thank you, Ken.

Shelley

Sixteen

Anxiety and the Workplace

THIS CHAPTER'S BIRTH was a direct result of inquiries from both employers and employees. Since there seemed to very little information about the subject available our group went to work gathering information. The material in this chapter comes from various sources but mostly from employees and employers. It is a real grassroots endeavor.

Shows extraordinary job commitment

Pays strong attention to details

Exhibits a high degree of selflessness

What employer wouldn't want an employee with these qualities?

Yet many mental health professionals agree that it is often people with these same perfectionist traits that have a tendency to suffer from panic and anxiety disorder (PAD). PAD manifests itself in sudden attacks of anxiety and may include such symptoms as trembling, difficulty breathing, rapid heartbeat, sweating, numbness and nausea. During an attack, the employee may fear she's having a heart attack or becomes so overwhelmed by panic that she feels compelled to escape to a place where she feels safe.

Workplace stress can initiate or heighten anxiety, but even tension outside the job sphere may harm the employee's performance. Ashamed of and isolated by the disorder, she is constantly terrorized by thoughts of having an attack at in the presence of a boss or coworkers.

So what can an employer do to retain a valuable employee and reduce the possibility of a workman's compensation or disability claim? According to mental health professionals, both employers and employees stand the best chance of surmounting problems arising from panic disorder if they educate themselves about the condition and communicate in good faith. Lack of candor on either side can be quite damaging in a business relationship. A worker who inflates what she's realistically capable of handling at the present time for fear of "letting the company down" may sabotage the relationship as much as the boss who agrees to lessen workplace tension and then continues to impose rigid deadlines.

"Part of the problem is distrust," says a former panic sufferer who works with others with the disorder. "For instance, a person with panic and anxiety went back to his job and was welcomed with open arms. Then he accidentally discovered they were keeping a file on him in preparation of firing him. That shattered him enough to put him back on sick leave and in a worse state than before."

With a variety of methods, including relaxation techniques, behavioral therapy and medicine, PAD is highly treatable. Therefore, the chances for a positive work outcome are high if both parties are willing to be honest, flexible and realistic. "I found what helped me most at work was the complete acceptance of my disorder," says an anxiety sufferer. "My co-workers asked me to explain it and what they should do if I started to feel uncomfortable. If I needed to leave the room in a hurry, they were very accepting. It only took a couple of weeks working in this atmosphere before I was very at ease at work and didn't have any problems."

Suggestions for Employers

1. Encourage the person with PAD to seek medical treatment first to rule out any underlying medical condition. If possible, put her in touch with the company's Human Resource Director or Employee Assistance Program.

2. Assure the PAD sufferer that it is fine to enlist a couple of co-workers with whom she feels comfortable to act as support givers in the event of distress. If she is dizzy or having trouble catching her breath, she may fear being alone.

3. Help her combat catastrophic thoughts by replacing them with positive ones. For instance, encourage her to change a thought like: "I'm going to collapse" to "I've never collapsed before, so there is no precedent that I'm going to collapse now."

4. Try to design assignments to maximize the PAD sufferer's effectiveness without adding additional stress. If there are jobs she can complete at home and that

is where she feels safe, perhaps in time of distress she may be allowed to work at home.

5. Don't insist that a worker with a social situation phobia attend lunch meetings in restaurants or staff parties that will increase her anxiety.

6. Discuss assignments with the affected worker before imposing them. Involve her in setting expectations.

7. Don't underestimate the healing power of compassion and compassionate humor. One employee with PAD says she and her co-workers laugh together each morning when they gather around the coffee maker and she is given only 1/2 cup of decaffeinated because they don't want to have to take her to the Dizzy Clinic. "For me," she says, "a serious approach with a touch of humor make my work environment a delightful place to be."

8. Understand that a worker with PAD may need to be excused from work-related travel or find someone to drive her to and from work or therapy appointments. PAD sufferers often avoid confined places such as automobiles, trains, busses, subways and airplanes. She fears being "trapped" in a location or setting from which "escape" may be difficult. She's also anxious about what other people will think of her if they witness her having an attack.

9. Invite an employee afflicted with PAD to make up her own First Aid Kit: a list of potential workplace remedies that can be realistically and readily adopted.

10. Don't treat the worker as if she's a child or her complaints are "made up" or "all in her head." PAD is a real disorder and it is estimated it affects some 15

million North Americans alone. Although a child can suffer from PAD, your worker is not one and deserves to be treated with dignity, the same as you would treat a worker with a chronic illness such as diabetes.

Considerations for the Workplace Environment

1. Warm fluorescent lights seem to help in place of cold fluorescents. The worker with PAD may benefit even if these lights are installed over just the one workstation.

2. Move an anxious employee's desk away from high-traffic and noisy locations.

3. Save a seat near a doorway in a meeting so the worker may exit the room quickly and unobtrusively if need be.

4. Music (classical, New Age, etc.) played at low volume can soothe frayed nerves. Allow the worker a place to keep and play a cassette deck if relaxation tapes are helpful.

5. Provide, if possible, a quiet, relatively private place where a worker can practice relaxation and breathing skills. A crowded "staff room" or public restroom are not appropriate settings.

A recent suggestion is, where possible, allow people to have flex-time, not just in terms of days but in terms of hours worked. This way they may be able to avoid being at work during times of the day they find very stressful.

When a person returns to work welcome them back as you would any other employee. Those recovering from heart attacks or other health problems are welcomed back with open arms. People recovering from anxiety, depression or any other similar disorder are frequently shunned.

Seventeen

Anxiety, Panic Attacks and the School Student

THIS MATERIAL HAS BEEN collated from the input of students, parents, teachers and health authorities. It is intended to be for informational purposes only. In no way does it purport to replace professional advice.

For the sake of clarity, the use of "she" has been adopted to include both "he" and "she."

Both students and school staff may suffer from anxiety and/or panic attacks. This section deals specifically with the student.

Any person suffering from a sudden onset of high anxiety or a panic attack is in distress. The natural impulse is to run to a safe place or, at least, from the present area. At home or in a store, rapid escape to a relatively safe place is possible. The more formal situation of the school presents problems. Can a student just get up and exit? What will the other students say or think? Can the student just leave the room or the school? What is the liability of the school if a student does exit on her own? What happens if a student has a panic attack in the middle of an exam? These, and others, are questions that were discussed with various groups of people. To some, there may no specific answer. To others, a number of suggestions or current policies are given.

It is unfortunate that several people reported they had had panic attacks for several months or longer without realizing what they were. In some cases the parents thought they were just going through a stage while the school believed them to be making it up and disciplined accordingly. On the opposite end, the school realized there was a problem and, working with the parents, identified it.

Once the problem had been identified the question of how to handle it comes to the fore. Various schools have handled it in different ways. Generally, the following procedure was used. The student was allowed to leave the room or remain in it depending upon how she felt. She may have felt comfortable just being quiet at her desk, going to a quiet part of the room or leaving the room. If the student left the room she could do so without obtaining permission but was required to proceed immediately to a place which she had identified as feeling "safe" to her. The safe place was usually where an adult was always present such as the office, the medical room or the custodial office.

Rules for actually leaving the premises differed considerably. Some school policies prevented this while others had made arrangements with the parents to take the student home even if the house were empty. Only in very severe cases was it necessary to take the student home. Normally she could rest for a while then return to the classroom.

What to tell the other students differed considerably from school to school and grade to grade. In consultation with the parents some schools told the class about the disorder and stressed that it was just like any other illness. Other schools left it to the student to tell some or all of her schoolmates. In most cases it was found that the classmates were very supportive and did what they could to help. In a very few cases it resulted in some teasing which only added to the burden.

Testing procedures also varied from school to school. Some allowed the student to write exams in a quiet room and some even went so far as to call a personal "time out" on the exam if the student began feeling stressed out. Other schools felt that no special considerations were given to students with other medical problems and none should be done so in this case.

Eighteen

Anxiety and the Law

T HIS SECTION FIRST APPEARED on my website over a year ago. It received many positive comments including that from Dr. Shipko.

> I find this of great interest. I have seen hundreds of people with lawsuits related to their panic disorder. First of all, as a State Qualified Examiner, Appellate level Social Security Disability evaluater, Disability Evaluater for the LAPD and a few hundred worker's compensation cases, expert testimony for both the insurance and the plaintiff—I think that people will benefit from your new website.
>
> Dr. S. Shipko, California

Synopsis
Due to the nature of Anxiety Disorders, those suffering from them can find themselves in almost impossible

situations when called upon to give evidence in courts, insurance appeals, before semi-judicious bodies and hearings of all types. This section gives a number of suggestions which have been found to be of use in helping these people through these stressful situations.

Background

Over the six years I have been maintaining this site, I have received numerous letters from people who were forced into these situations and suffered severely. The plea from them was, "Please publish this so others will not have to go through it." Recently I have begun to receive feedback which indicates that at least some of the people in authority are beginning to understand and are taking steps to see that those with anxiety disorders are not further traumatized during the hearings, giving of evidence, etc. Many of these people find it difficult, if not impossible, to do many of the fun things they did prior to the onset of their disability. House parties, small gatherings, walks through malls, etc., can now produce so much anxiety and/or fear that they must be avoided. In extreme cases their safe zones have become so restricted they cannot leave the house. Their lives are now centered around avoiding stressful situations.

While many are forced to function within these limitations, it does not mean they have given up striving for improvement or complete recovery. They are generally working daily to try to overcome the fear-based restrictions that have been placed upon them. Some will heal in a few months; others may take years. Depending upon where they are in the healing process, some will be able to take virtually no stress, others can take a little, while others will find it uncomfortable but are able to pull through—and all points in between. To push them too much beyond their limits could well set them back. The harm may not show immediately but they and their families could be faced with months or years of hardships from the resulting damage.

As they cannot handle the normal daily stress, a forced adversarial meeting such as in courtrooms, hearings, insurance appeals, etc., is devastating to them. It can be so devastating to them that a number cannot even pursue insurance appeals—they just have to give up and walk away. (Unfortunately, it seems that a number of agencies, being aware of this, draw events out as long as possible.)

So what can be done to help these people?

Ideally, what they need is a non-threatening situation in which they feel they are in control regarding location, setting the pace, leaving, selecting seats near doors, etc. Below are a number of things which have been tried with success. Of course not all suggestions will be possible, nor will everyone require as much support. Who is the best person to ask what type of support they need? The person with the disorder!

Before the Event

Allow the person to walk through the empty room, noting the position of doors, etc.

Explain the nature of the proceedings, who sits where, and estimated time lines.

Make it clear the person may leave by any door at any time. They probably won't have to leave, but knowing the option is there can be beneficial.

Ask what can be done to make them feel more comfortable.

Assure them they may bring a support person with them and that they will not be on their own.

Officers of the court and major players should be made aware of the disorder and any restrictions that must be made for their "mental" protection should be discussed.

Since these people are fear-based, it is not unusual to find that the person has an unreasonable fear of retaliation from anyone they give evidence against.

Ask the person what would make her feel more comfortable.

If one of their requests cannot be met, try to work out a compromise.

During the Event

The person is a witness; do not keep her in a small isolation room from which she cannot leave. Being trapped is a big part of panic attacks. Certainly, don't keep the person there alone.

Make sure the person is not seated so that she looks out a window that is high off the ground.

If the person must be in a witness stand, it should not be isolated or off the ground. In fact, it may be easier to just have the person sitting in a regular chair at a table with other people. Some have found that a conference room table with people sitting around it is much less stressful. The less they feel the center of attention, the better it is.

It may be necessary to have the caregiver sitting very close to the person while she gives testimony. This gives them a safe anchor.

It is frequently not possible to tell if the person is having a panic attack or an almost uncontrollable desire to run. Either the caregiver should be relied upon to make the decision or else those in charge may gently and quietly ask from time to time if the person is OK. However, in some, asking the person if she is OK can bring on an attack. It is obviously best to have worked something out ahead of time.

External signs of panic attack *may* include, sweating, a change of pallor, not seeming to be with it, being very snappy. Most can be very subtle and the caregiver who knows the person well may be the only person to recognize the rise in anxiety to the point of almost not functioning.

However, many people with anxiety disorders do extremely well giving testimony when their anxiety is high. The problem is recognizing "mental" exhaustion. How long does that take? It varies from person to person but my own experience with people would indicate that about 3/4 of an hour is the limit for many. Again, this is extremely variable from person to person. It may just be a few minutes or over an hour.

By their very nature, many people with anxiety are perfectionists. They will not forgive themselves for making small mistakes. Catastrophizing the results of the mistake can occupy them for a very long period of time. It is, therefore, important to be sure that the person is not in too high a state of anxiety. When they are in a high state they can almost be in a state of dissociation and may agree with almost any statement made to them. Later, when the anxiety level lowers they will realize they agreed but knew that it was incorrect and either will want to correct the statement or, if they can-

not, they will be haunted by it for some time. During
this time they can sound very confused and may even
appear to be contradictory.

In short, the adversarial system may not be one in
which they can freely give of their knowledge. The person in charge must make certain the "witness is not
being badgered."

As One Person Put It to Me

"Damn it! If I had a broken foot they would not allow
someone to keep irritating it. But, because I have an anxiety disorder, no one stops them from using it against me.

Those Severely Disabled by Anxiety Disorders

Some people are so severely disabled with anxiety disorders they may not be able to function at all outside of
their safe zones. Some are even confined to their homes.

In cases such as this various officials have found it
necessary to treat them just they would anyone else
who was too sick to attend. Meeting at the home, video-
taping, etc. have all been used.

Sometimes it is not necessary to go that extreme.
Finding a meeting place within their safe zone, changing the location of a hearing, court case or appeal to a
room on the bottom floor, have all been found to be
beneficial. It is really a matter of discussion with the
person, practicality, understanding, and compassion.

A Few Footnotes

Depression can frequently accompany anxiety. People
should be aware it can also be present and is an additional limiting factor.

A problem with juries has been noted. The manner in which these people may give their testimony has been interpreted by jury members as "not being sure," "stretching the truth," "outright lies," etc.

The adrenaline flow that occurs during high anxiety frequently causes the person to be very tired. After an appearance they will probably be sleeping for the next few days and/or worrying big time that the car may have been going at 55 and not the 60 they indicated. Therefore, having them return to give further testimony may not be a realistic option.

People with anxiety disorders are frequently peacemakers and people pleasers. They do not want (as opposed to need) to be treated any differently from anyone else. As a result of this, they will frequently attempt to go far beyond their capabilities.

In addition to being snappy, a person may become angry. This is a redirection from anxiety to another type of outlet. While a person may exhibit anger, there is no excuse whatsoever for the person to be rude or insulting.

It is unfortunate that some people use the anxiety problem to their benefit by making them sound confused. I have little that is polite to say to these people but there is a flip side. I have been amazed how the person's behavior can change when they become really angry. In some cases they have suddenly shown the sharp clear minds they normally have and cut the feet out from someone who thought they had them to the point of near self-destruction.

Likewise, I can think of no term to describe some disability insurance companies who insist that to pursue the claim for being housebound with agoraphobia, they must present themselves at some place that there is no hope of them being able to attend. In one case when a court order was issued to have the hearing at the person's house, the insurance company appealed it.

There is one school of thought which claims people with an anxiety disorder can attend a meeting anywhere and can be treated as any other person. The person may be able to force herself to do it but the down stream damage can be long lasting and severe.

In Summary

The above is not a Christmas wish list. They are suggestions from people who tried the various "aids" to help those with anxiety. The severity of disorder and the degree of accommodation vary from person to person. Certainly not all of the above will apply to everyone or even anyone. It should be done on an individual basis through discussion with the person and her caregiver.

Finally

I would like to end with a cute excerpt I received from a very frustrated court officer who was looking for a solution. It seems a crime was committed in front of a group of people who were just leaving an anxiety support group meeting. Most of them had extreme difficulties in giving evidence.

The court officer's email contained the following:

> Here come de judge,
> Here come de judge.
> There go de witnesses,
> There go de witnesses.

Nineteen

I Get Blamed and Yelled at So Much

WE HAVE ALL BEEN IN situations where a person who is upset, behind schedule or stressed lashes out by yelling or blaming. "How do you expect me to get it done when you keep butting in?" We probably just accept that the person is having a bad day and get out of the way.

A couple of years ago a person on my Internet caregivers' group expressed the concern that he was being blamed and yelled at frequently by his wife who had an anxiety disorder. As is frequently the case, several others on the group responded by saying they were in a similar situation but had had no idea they were not alone.

Why Does a Person Act this Way?

Jean, who has an anxiety disorder, responded to the group with her feelings.

As a person with anxiety who does at times lose it and start to blame my spouse I can offer the following possible reasons. It usually happens when I am feeling overwhelmed by responsibilities and do not feel supported by my husband. Often he withdraws to look after his own problems just when I feel especially vulnerable. I have to chase after him and ask for help or attention and this is humiliating. I get angry after feeling hurt and uncared for.

Some days it's just too much to suffer in silence and we lash out. We try to do all we can on our own with what definitely seems like inferior coping skills and nerves that are exhausted yet are supposed to be calm and not overreact when we are driven up the wall.

Presumably the caregiver could always leave, which is one of the common fears of people with anxiety (abandonment). I, however, have often wondered why they stay and what benefits they get out of such an "unequal " relationship. I don't think many caregivers are very self reflective but the ones with anxiety certainly are and do take more of their share of responsibility for any conflicts in a relationship.

Jean

Jean raised a number of points in her letter. She feels:
- overwhelmed,
- a lack of support,
- neglected,
- humiliated at having to ask for help and attention,
- she lacks effective coping skills.

Jean also raised some other points common among those with anxiety, including the fear of abandonment, and a feeling of being unworthy of being loved and cared for. The fearful question is "Why does he stay with me when I act this way?"

If read from a certain bias, Jean's letter could indicate all of the problems are caused by her. That is not true, of course; two people living together in such an environment are bound to bounce off each other's actions. Certainly being a support person does not imply we walk on water and do no wrong. However we can make just as many mistakes as the next person— and probably more when we are getting strung out. Sure, we make mistakes, but some of the time support people are unjustifiably blamed/attacked/criticized by the anxious person.

For the sake of clarification I have divided "blame" into five categories.

1. You did it and goofed badly.

    You did and goofed badly. "David, you promised to help me go Christmas shopping today and now you told Liam you would meet him at the pub." Oops! Time to cancel with Liam, and try to assure your partner she really does count. Don't forget the *sincere* apology. From reading the above you can see you just triggered several of her fears and impressions of herself such as unworthiness and having to beg for attention. Don't forget many with anxiety have possibly experienced many disappointments and broken promises.

2. You did it but there was no harm intended. You may not feel you even did anything wrong...it normally would not be an issue.

Have you ever been told, "I know I could have driven to the store if only you had not left the car radio on. It blasted me out of my seat when I turned on the ignition. I am too upset now to go."?

3. You did it (maybe) but the event is so minor it normally should not be an issue.

"I was all set to phone about the plumbing bill but you took the pen away from the phone. You know these things upset me. Now I am too shaky to phone."

4. You know you didn't do it.

"You left the clothes washer taps on again. It could have flooded us out." You have not been near it and you may even be hard pressed to recall precisely where the washer and dryer live.

5. Being blamed for the person having anxiety or for them thinking they are not making much progress —or for even having setbacks.

"How do you expect me to get better when you are acting that way? Maybe I am going to have to leave."

Unfortunately, in a world where fear, stress, anxiety, guilt, lack of confidence and, low self-esteem rule, blaming can be common. Without all parties working towards it, this is likely to happen. Prevention of blaming and feelings of guilt can be one of your shared goals.

It would be positive for the whole family if blame were not raised. Instead of, "You did it!", something like, "I found the laundry taps on. Let's double check them after we use the washer."

What Can You do About it? Other people posting responses to the question on blaming offered some suggestions.

It is *never* acceptable to be treated as a door-mat. Whenever my husband and I have a situation like this, whether it is from my anxiety or his anger, we say something like, I'm not going to talk to you when you are like this and we walk away. We may have to repeat ourselves a few times but eventually, the other gets the picture and we have some time to cool down.

There is no excuse for treating anyone in the manner described. Regardless of the situation, medically, or otherwise—In a case like that, where it may be due to medication or anxiety, the other person must help to take the initiative to walk away or take a positive action to stop the behavior. Be consistent and be ready to repeat yourself. It's like teaching a child in a way. We must teach by example. We also learn by example.

If you are a support person you are possibly the frequent target of the anxious person's frustration. Is it right to just accept it? Should you respond? If you do respond, how? This question was also put out to the support group for comment.

All respondents noted you certainly do not have to take it. Perhaps you both could make a positive growth experience from it by addressing it together or with a counselor.

While many pointed out it was not correct to accept it, a number suggested you not have too thin a skin and if the problem were minor just forget it.

Being Criticized

Many support people complain that they are constantly criticized for the way in which they do things. This can be anything from handling family finances to setting the table.

Recently I received a question from someone who was constantly being told he was doing things wrong. In the case he used as an example it was trying to help with dinner by peeling the carrots. His wife became very upset with him and insisted he was peeling the carrots incorrectly. I put up the following question on my Internet group for caregivers.

"You are making supper. Out of the blue comes a command," That is not the way you peel carrots. You start at the little end." As the caregiver to someone whose anxiety is obviously very high, what would you do? Keep peeling, change ends, walk away, suggest she read *Gulliver's Travels?*"

A number of people posted their ideas. I have put two below.

I will give my immediate thought that I had to your question, I don't know the correctness, but would appreciate the learning.

...The carrots obviously need to be peeled and I would say to the command that "I will try the other way and see which is easier for me," and continue to peel carrots.

My personal reasoning being that it is only a carrot and not really worth a fight which would increase the anxiety levels present at that time. If it were genuinely easier I would change anyway. My personal belief being that if someone offers advice, take it on board. If it helps, use it; and if not, put the advice aside.

Does that make sense?

This second response came from a woman who has recovered from anxiety but assists others by sharing her experiences.

"I think as a person with a/p we are really too picky with how things are done, but that is part of the disorder. I agree, with the other post, try it that way, and then do it the way you want, when they are not looking.

Perfectionism is so much a part of the disorder. It really takes a lot of patience to deal with us. I remember doing the same thing to my daughter about how to fix carrots for cooking. LOL Really hit home. Now that I have recovered, I really practice not being so picky and letting things slide. As far as being the caregiver, do the best you can at pleasing them, but don't let them rule you. There is a really fine line and crossing it can just make the ill person worse. I really believe in boundaries. Hope this helps."

Both people adopted a non-aggressive approach but made it clear they had their way of doing things. This would be called the "assertive method."

Broadly speaking there are three different types of response behavior recognized for such situations.

A. Aggressive

The underlying tendency of the aggressive response is based on the person's belief that he is always right, his needs are more important than those of others' and, he will stand for nothing which removes his feelings of superiority.

B. Passive

Just the opposite of aggressive. This person believes

his feelings are less important than those of others. He
will not openly challenge another person's opinion. In
fact, he may even apologize for 'always being wrong."
Neither A nor B are healthy responses.

C. Assertive

This person believes his ideas and needs are just
as important as anyone elses. He will stand up for
himself but leaves the door open for others to
express contrary opinions. This person tries to find
some common solution but does not feel compelled
to respond immediately. He will say clearly that he is
going to think about the situation. He does not walk
out slamming the door but, instead, explains polite-
ly what he is doing. Then he makes sure he does get
back after he has thought about it.

With a little practice, assertiveness should work in
most situations. However, remember you are dealing
with someone whose fear and anxiety is probably off
the scale so give a bit of slack.

Some people who have not lived in an anxiety driven
situation may feel the example of peeling carrots incorrectly was an exaggeration. Not one person on the caregivers' list raised an eyebrow at the example. Several
responded with other examples, which, to the uninformed, would seem just as trivial.

There is one point of which you should be aware.
After a period of time being blamed, yelled at, and criticized, it is very easy for the caregiver to slip into either
the aggressive or passive response.

If you do happen to blow up, apologize and move on.
We are all human.

You may recall I ended my original question with,

"Keep peeling, change ends, walk away, suggest she read *Gulliver's Travels?*" The suggestion that she read *Gulliver's Travels* would have been a terrible response ...pure sarcasm which is not helpful. (In his travels Gulliver came across two cities that were at war over the question of the correct way to open an egg...big end first or little end first.)

Several people have written to say that when they have a disagreement with someone who is very uptight and *must* convince the caregiver, the anxious person speaks with such certainty and uses so many points to make her case, it all sounds very logical and correct. Later when the caregiver thinks about it, he realizes that there are many holes in the argument but it seemed so good at the time. Yes, those with anxiety are very good at it. One wag on our Internet group called this the "politicians' syndrome." But just to be clear, I am not saying those with anxiety have flawed logic. Just the opposite. On the whole they are very intelligent people. I am just referring here to those situations in which a person must have their way. e.g., We shouldn't go to the movie tonight because..." The person does not want to admit she is just too frightened to go and so presents an excellent reason.

Main Points

- A person who is very anxious may resort to yelling, blame and criticism.
- The caregiver is not required to take it.
- Do not accept it, but do not reply in the same manner.
- The assertive method is the best for resolving disagreements.

Twenty

Frequently Asked Questions

SOME OF THESE QUESTIONS were raised in other chapters but it does not hurt to mention them again.

Are anxiety and panic attacks new?

No. They were described in medical literature over 100 years ago.

Are they becoming more common?

It seems so, but it could be due to better diagnosis, a greater public awareness and more available information. Some think our more stressful lifestyle is a contributing factor. Statistically about 15% of the population will suffer from some form of anxiety illness in their lifetime. Some will seek treatment, some will get over it themselves. Some will just suffer and others will turn to alcohol, and perhaps other drugs, to try to find relief.

Do men and women both develop anxiety illnesses?

Yes, but more women than men seem to develop them —or at least seek treatment. Men, more commonly than women, turn to alcohol for relief, and are less likely to seek treatment.

Can people of any age develop anxiety illnesses?

Yes.

Are people with anxiety illnesses sane?

Absolutely. However, until diagnosed and reassured, it is not uncommon for these people to feel they are becoming insane.

Why do they feel they are becoming insane?

On an intellectual level they know there is no external cause to feel anxious or panicky but they do and it is just as real to them as it would be to a person in a genuinely dangerous situation. The same is true of those with OCD and PTSD; what they feel bears little resemblance to reality but to them it is real and they are forced to respond in the manner they do.

Can't they just shrug it off and realize it is all in the mind?

Once diagnosed, they realize it is "all in the mind"[2] but they can't just shrug it off because the body won't stop reacting the way it does. Even with OCDs the fearful

---

2 This is meant to include the biochemistry of the brain.

consequences of not carrying out the "ritual" outweigh the knowledge that it is not natural.

Why do they keep looking for other causes even after being diagnosed?

Some fear the stigma that (to some extent) still goes with a mental illness and feel a need to find another cause. Others need to find they have an illness that can be fixed quickly with a pill. Still others just won't accept that their minds can deceive them to such an extent. Part of the job of a support person is to gently help them to accept that they have an anxiety illness. Once that is settled effective treatment may begin.

Why is depression common in these people?

They are not in control of their situation. Their intellect tells them one thing but the body does another. Not being in control, never knowing when another attack may hit, and being restricted in their lifestyle for reasons they don't fully understand, can lead to the depression. Also, recent research has shown that similar reactions in the brain may account for both anxiety and depression. Perhaps there is a common cause for both.

Is there nothing they can do to control this?

No, in the short run. They are slaves to the anxiety. In the long run they can be helped by medication and a change in thinking patterns.

Well, aren't they overreacting?

No. They are reacting "normally" for the situation.

Imagine you are trapped in a room with a cobra slith-
ering in the door and there is nothing you can do. Now
take away the cobra but keep the panic feelings and
you have something similar to their experience.

Do anxious people act "normal"?

That depends upon what you mean by normal and/or
the severity of the symptoms. A person who is anxious
may just seem to be uptight a lot of the time. They
may ask that you do things in a certain way without
having a rational explanation (e.g. cut the lawn from
right to left) because they have a fear that all will not
be well if it is not done that way. They may ask you to
drive back to the house because they "forgot something" where, in reality, they just need to check the
stove one more time.

Why do they try to hide the real reason?

So you won't think they are nuts. There is also a great
deal of shame associated with the way they react. Many
with anxiety illnesses are in such mental pain they
can't or don't want to explain.

What other reasons prevent a person from revealing her illness?

The perceived stigma of a mental/emotional illness, the
possibility of job loss, and not letting your enemies or
competitors know your weak points, are some of the
additional reasons. Others may be privacy, fear of how
your friends and family will react, etc.

I feel I am betraying my wife if I reach out for help. She does not want to say anything to anyone.

This is a common feeling amongst those who have reached the end of their rope and reach out for help. There is nothing wrong with looking after yourself. The "conspiracy of silence" in a family can frequently lead to illness in other family members and put an unnecessary stress on the family unit. It is selfish for a person to ask for all the help but not allow you to get any. I think this is one of the times you can be excused for not remaining silent when you need the help.

What is meant by 'mental pain'?

It is very private pain coming from within. You can be hurt by someone letting you down or insulting you, but that does not begin to describe the mental torture these people are going through on the inside due to anguish, despair, frustration, disappointment, fear, and hopelessness. It is something one talks about only to trusted people whom they hope will understand and not rebuff their confidences.

What is negative self-talk?

That is the little voice inside the head which is constantly telling the person they are no good, they screwed up again, made a fool of themselves, should have done it another way. During the healing process this type of talk has to be replaced with positive self-talk. The "should haves" and "if onlys" have to be replaced with phrases like, "so what," "does it really matter?" "I am worthy of being loved," "I love myself." "We all make mistakes." A support person should emphasize the positive and attempt to eliminate the negative self-talk.

Does the person usually have a negative self-image?

Many do, and if they didn't have one when they started with the anxiety they often develop one. The support person should try to help to build up the self-image, but the image improvement has to come from within the person.

What is anticipatory anxiety?

It's rather like stage fright which some actors experience before going on stage. The actor overcomes it and goes out onto the stage. In the case of people with panic attacks the stage is the area outside their safe zones. They have an anxiety that they may have a panic attack. If they do not leave their safe zone due to the anticipatory anxiety, they have developed agoraphobia.

What is the difference between an anxiety attack and a panic attack?

The person with high anxiety frequently (or almost constantly) feels as if something threatening is going to happen—they don't know what—just an uneasy feeling. An anxiety attack occurs when the level of anxiety suddenly increases to the point where a person virtually cannot function. A panic attack is quite different. A person may feel fine, and then the panic attack begins out of the blue. A feeling of a rising adrenaline level rapidly climbs to the point where the person is not in control of her body. Little distinction was made between the two in the text of this book because, as the support person, you respond similarly.

Do all people with anxiety/panic attacks show the same symptoms?

No. Some may be perfectly all right driving while others have a terrible time. The same is true of various other situations.

How is this illness treated?

Usually with a combination of drugs and counselling.

Will the person ever get over the illness?

Yes. For some it takes more time than others but they will. They may never have the symptoms again or there may be the odd twinge for up to a few years later. The important thing is for the person not to allow the symptoms of a twinge to re-trigger the fears that led to the full blown attacks. Being prepared for the odd twinge is better than believing that it was the absolute end. It is much too easy to fall back into the old thought patterns if they are not prepared to use their coping mechanisms at any time—even years down the road.

What are panic attacks like?

Try to explain to a man what being pregnant is like. Unless you have been there it is difficult to understand. Have you ever been so frightened that you panicked and just wanted to get out of the situation? If you have been in this situation you know the adrenaline starts flowing as it prepares you to fight or run. Your heart speeds up, your breathing rate increases and you are just plain scared and want out. Once you have left the danger zone and found a safe place your body starts returning to normal. With panic attacks this same response is triggered off, frequently with no apparent cause.

What does a person with a panic disorder feel?

Common symptoms are pounding heart, chest pains, light-headedness or dizziness, nausea or stomach problems, flushes or chills, shortness of breath or feelings of choking, tingling or numbness shaking or trembling, feelings of unreality, terror, feelings of being out of control or going crazy, fear of dying.

What can be done about the burning sensation in the chest?

This burning sensation is noticed by a number of people when their anxiety level is very high and is frequently mistaken for a heart attack. It is due to the effect the stress is having on the chest muscles. If the muscles are pinched by grabbing them with your hand, the burning may subside briefly. This at least shows it is in the muscles and not the heart. I have found that the use of a warm/hot damp cloth on the chest will frequently relieve the pain.

Why are many people who have panic attacks unable to enter elevators, stand in bank lines, walk between high shelves in grocery stores, etc.?

They feel trapped with no easily available exit. Anticipatory anxiety frequently prevents them from putting themselves in such situations

What is agoraphobia?

If a person becomes uncomfortable or develops panic attacks when they leave the house or a certain part of the house, then agoraphobia is present. It is very difficult, if not impossible for them to venture very far from their comfortable area or safe spot.

What is a support person?

Some people refer to a "caregiver"; I prefer "support person." A caregiver, to me, is someone giving help to a terminally ill person. People with anxiety illnesses are not terminally ill, but many wish they could be. The support person is the person (or people) the anxious person turns to for help. They trust the support person to aid them entering into scary situations and not to let them down. Some books say the relationship between the support person and the anxious person is rather like that between a frightened child and a loving, supportive parent.

Must the support person be a very well adjusted and trained counselor?

No. If the support person has a few small problems it can be a time for both to get over their problems together. This is true, particularly, in a family situation where the ill person turns to the spouse.

What is meant by "enabling"?

This is the action of helping someone perform or carry out an undesirable act which is based on the person's anxiety disorder. For instance, if a person has OCD and "can't" touch any laundry, an enabler would do the laundry for the person.

Is the family to blame for the person having this?

Not likely. That gets us back into the chapter on causes that really came to no conclusion. What is important is that the family examine itself in a positive way so they may all pull together to help the person overcome the illness.

Is the person at fault for having an anxiety disorder?

No. They are no more at fault for having an anxiety disorder than they would be at fault for developing, say, diabetes.

If the body is designed for fight or flight why does it develop problems?

The body is designed to react to events and then return to normal. It has not evolved to be able to be at a high state of alertness for long periods of time.

Can the person control the attack?

With understanding and the development of key actions or thoughts the attack *may* be abated. This all takes time to learn from reading, counselling, etc.

After my friend takes a course to help his anxiety even if we have opposite viewpoints on a small matter he keeps saying, "My feelings count too."

Give him time. He is relearning to have confidence in himself. It may take awhile for his social skills to return so that he can use these phrases correctly.

How long does it take to overcome an anxiety illness?

It depends on the person and the type of help she is getting. For some, drugs alone may do it; for others the drugs may give the person a jump-start on the road to recovery, but it can take weeks, months or years. Fortunately methods of treatment are becoming better and intervention can occur earlier, but the time it takes really varies from person to person.

How do we find someone who is trained in anxiety illnesses?

It is becoming easier than it was just a couple of years ago. Try the local hospital or Psychology Dept. of a nearby university. If there are self-help groups in the area ask at those meetings.

What is expected of a support person?

The role varies depending upon ground rules agreed upon. The support person should be the strong arm on which the ill person can lean. They may have to act as a driver or stand by the telephone if the person is entering a threatening situation on her own. The support person should be willing to listen to the ill person as they talk about their feelings. It is usually not welcomed to be judgmental. Phrases like, "You know that is ridiculous," "Don't be silly," almost always do more harm than good. The anxious persons' feelings are very real to them. They know they are not being rational but can't help it. You don't have to agree with them but neither should their perceptions be strongly knocked. That they feel sufficiently comfortable with you to share the feelings indicates the trust they have put in you. Their change in outlook must come from within and that takes time.

What is not expected of a support person?

A support person is not expected to be a butler, a servant or a slave. Neither is the support person expected to give so much that they too become ill.

Isn't being a support person a very responsible function?

Yes, but it can also a very rewarding function. Spouses frequently find that as the panic attacks subside, they have grown closer together and understand each other more. Similarly, entire families sometimes feel they have grown much closer together.

Can more than one person be a support person?

Certainly. If several people in a family and friends work together, all the better. In fact, for the sake of the support people, it is highly desirable that there be more than one.

They don't talk to me much about what they are thinking.

Give them time. Your role is support and to be a good listener if they feel like talking.

How can I help if they don't tell me what they talked about with their counselor?

What they say to their counselor is really none of your business. You have your role, the counselors have theirs.

I think it would be better if I could talk to her doctor.

The type of response you get from the doctor will vary. They may listen or not choose to listen. They may report what you said back to the patient. Remember their first responsibility is to the patient and they are bound by their oath not to discuss their patient with anyone else unless they have permission from the patient. If you think it is really important, talk it over with the anxious person but don't feel slighted if she does not wish to give permission. She is just doing whatever makes them the most comfortable.

What is a safe place?

If a person is restricted in her movements by panic attacks and/or agoraphobia she probably has places where she feels safe. They may be large areas like the whole neighborhood or very small ones like the bedroom. It is very difficult and threatening for her to leave these places.

What happens when they leave their safe zone?

They tend to become very anxious and full-blown panic attacks may occur.

Are safe places always in the house?

Not always. There may be other safe areas such as in the office or in a car.

How often do panic attacks occur?

From one every few years to several times a day.

Can you tell if a person is having a panic attack?

In many cases no. They look and act as though nothing is wrong. However, in the midst of a panic attack, they may suddenly have to bolt for the nearest exit without regard to anything else.

How long do the attacks last?

Some experts insist only a few minutes but those that have them report they last from a few minutes to several hours or even longer.

Why is the person tired after an attack?

The body has used up a fair amount of energy just as it would in a "real" emergency.

Is there another way a person can look at the panic attack?

Many people fear the arrival of the next attack. However, several of those who have made a recovery have come to look on the attacks as nothing more that a severe stomach ache. They know it is not life threatening and just let it wash over them—it will pass.

What is the DSM IV I keep hearing about?

The DSM IV is the fourth edition of the Diagnostic Statistical Manual of Mental Disorders. It is a publication for use by professionals that gives the criteria for diagnosing and classifying the various mental disorders. You may find it listed as DSM VI (REV), which is a year 2000 update.

What is the ICD 10?

This stands for the International Classification of Diseases that is put out by the World Health Organization. It is used internationally to classify diseases and disorders including mental disorders. Some diagnostic criteria are slighting different to those in the DSM.

What are some things I should not say to an anxious person?

We have discussed a number in the book such as, "It is all in your head." "What is the matter with you?" Even when trying to be helpful there are some pitfalls. One of the major ones is, "I know exactly how you feel." This is a statement that leaves them nothing much more to say even when they are trying to discuss their feelings with you.

What should I do if the family is in denial or doesn't want to help or understand?

There is little you can do. Just recognize the additional pain this is causing the ill person.

What should the children be told?

The truth. Not to do so could leave them wondering all their lives why mother never bothered to go to see them play sports or visit the school, and could lead to the child's interpretation that the parent doesn't care. Children are surprisingly receptive and understanding. See if they have a role they can play in helping their mother. Of course the ill person should still show interest in their daily lives outside the home. Videos, pictures, tape recordings and conversations will allow all the family to share events.

Are there things I can do when I leave a very anxious person alone?

First enjoy the time you have on your own. Also, it helps if you leave them something to do, such as plenty of crosswords or fun sewing.

Why does the anxious person in our house always seem to be the first to notice new sounds or smells?

They usually are the first. Possibly because they are running more on the "speed up" system which makes them hypervigilant.

Isn't it a balancing act between encouraging the person to go out and pushing her too hard?

Yes.

How about pets?

Pets seem to be of great help to some.

Any tips for grocery stores?

Pushing the cart seems to give the person something to focus on.

Can house decoration play a role?

Yes. If it is impossible to go on holidays some find it helpful to paint holiday scenes on the walls or put up posters, etc. The use of restful and healing colors on the walls also helps.

How about gardening?

Some people find this to be very relaxing therapy.

The person seems to have great difficulty making decisions.

Yes, they do. They are intelligent and can see many sides to a question but the anxiety prevents them from coming to a conclusion. Recently I was contacted by a man who had watched his retirement savings disappear in the recent bear market. For two years he wanted to convert from stocks to cash but was afraid the markets would turn around. So, for the two years he was frozen into immobility by fear and a lack of self-confidence.

The number of social invitations we receive is dropping.

Frequently phoning at the last minute to cancel your attendance at social events can have this effect over time. Those who are up front and explain the problem report a much better understanding than those who just "keep developing headaches."

My partner develops anxiety when returning to our home and I am beginning to think this means I am the cause of her anxiety.

If it has been a particularly tumultuous relationship— maybe. But there are other possible explanations. The person has probably had many PAs at home and is beginning to subconsciously associate the home with them. Also, some suggest it may have its roots in the past if, as a child, they returned home every day to a very unhappy situation.

It hurts when I hear comments like, "Be careful. If anything happened to you, who would take care of me?" Does she mean that is all I am good for?

Probably not in the way it sounds. You may have just heard one of her basic fears being expressed.

Some people with anxiety seem to be forgetful.

This is true of both those with anxiety and with depression. Either the information is not being stored or else it is not being retrieved.

I notice my wife gets tired very easily.

Anxiety, itself, takes energy. It requires energy to be alert, tremble or show any of the other symptoms.

A number of people with anxiety seem to be afraid of abandonment.

This is true but whether or not it is any greater in people with anxiety than those without, I don't know.

A number of people with anxiety seem to be afraid of rejection.

This is true but whether or not it is any greater in people with anxiety than those without, I don't know.

A number of people with anxiety seem to come from dysfunctional families.

This is true but whether or not it is any greater in people with anxiety than those without, I don't know. Also, this is a chicken and egg question. Do they have anxiety because of their backgrounds or do the genes for anxiety exist in the family?

I sometimes get frustrated.

Yes, well—we are all human. Remember, this is a mutual working together and understanding relationship.

Do men and women both develop anxiety disorders?

Yes, but more women than men seem to develop them —or at least seek treatment. Men, more commonly

than women, turn to alcohol for relief, and are less likely to seek treatment.

I seem to get yelled at a lot

The anxious person is very uptight, frustrated, angry,
and has a lot of emotional energy to dispose of. Many
women describe it as feeling crankier than during a bad
case of PMS. You don't have to take it. Tell them you
don't appreciate it and, if necessary, leave the area for
a short while. Remember you are not a doormat, but
don't have too thin a skin.

My wife seems to be worse just after she has wakened up.

This is common. The body goes through a number of
chemical changes when it changes from sleep to being
awake. Remember these people respond with anxiety
to events that would have little to no effect on us.

Why do the attacks seem to come out of the blue?

Good question. Do we have a good answer? Not really.
It has been suggested that since they respond with an
anxiety response to stimuli we may not even notice,
they may be reacting to a temperature change, a flow of
adrenaline from excitement, a change of light, or
maybe the body just does it on its own without external stimuli.

My girl friend insists on walking down a busy street by herself even though she feels like she

is going to have a panic attack. I am worried she is doing harm.

It will be beneficial to her. She is desensitizing herself and building up confidence.

Anything else? Much, but two points immediately spring to mind. 1) Bring fun into the life of the ill person. If she can't get out then rent videos, have friends visit, etc. 2) Take care of yourself. You will be of no use to anyone if you wear out or become so centered on the person with anxiety you lose your own friends, interests and yourself.

What is codependency?

The last sentence of the above questions just touches on codependency, "...become so centered on the person with anxiety you lose your own friends, interests and yourself." Codependency is an illness which may become obvious in caregivers who have a tendency towards it. If you find it happening to you, discuss the situation with a professional before you are so completely swallowed up by it, it becomes your "normal" lifestyle. However, you may find what you are doing and feeling is not codependency given the circumstances of living with a person who has anxiety. Check it out to make sure. That is "check it out." Don't jump to conclusions and ruin a normal relationship.

Some codependency traits to watch for:
• Feeling good about myself stems from being liked by you.

- I need your approval before I can feel good about myself.
- I have put aside my own interests and hobbies to share your interests and hobbies.
- I have lost my friends but I prefer to flutter around you.
- I have no time or interest to know how I feel. I am centered on how you feel.
- All my dreams for the future center on you.
- I look at you as a reflection of myself and so control how you dress, act, etc. I really have no image of myself as an individual.
- The quality of my life depends upon the quality of yours.
- I am so busy with your wants, feelings and hurts, I don't feel I exist anymore as an individual. But that is OK.

Why do they seem to talk in blanket statements when talking about problems?

This is part of the thinking pattern which must be changed. Problems and errors are magnified. For instance, "Everything goes wrong for me." "You always screw up." "Things are always going wrong with my car." "I can't get anything right anymore." "I can't trust you to buy the right groceries so I have to do it. Just something else on my list of things I have to do." Perhaps a tad of perfectionism here too. They demand very high standards of themselves and become frustrated when others on whom they have to rely do not share the need for perfectionism. Of course, this perfectionism may well be one of the triggers which contributed to the anxiety disorder.

What do people fear the most: physiological or psychological symptoms of panic attacks?

The information given here was supplied by Dr. Stone of the U.K. from unpublished research which she kindly sent to me to use.

The research project involved 432 responses to a questionnaire on the Internet. The physiological symptoms include such things as heart palpitations, chest pains, etc. The psychological symptoms include the strange disorientating feelings people have during a panic attack. These psychological symptoms are the ones which make people feel they are losing their minds and out of control. Of the 432 respondents, 164 (38%) said they suffered from both the physiological and the psychological symptoms. Of these 164 peoples, 160 (96%) said they feared the psychological symptoms the most.

Dr. Stone went on to say,

"This is very important as most doctors treat physiological symptoms of panic attacks and somehow feel that psychological symptoms are akin to mental illness, or 'pull yourself together, it is all in your mind' and so the importance of [the] real problem is missed. There is no question that 'losing one's mind' is a frightening experience, and moreover, in this preliminary research there is a strong tendency towards the [usually] assertive personalities to have these psychological symptoms. This makes it more frightening as loss of control to those personality types is very important in any case."

Any other advice?

The people with anxiety disorders are very courageous as they do their best to carry on despite the anguish, mental pain and debilitation. The support people play an important role in the lives of these ill people and also deserve credit for the services they perform and roles they play.

Twenty-one

Ashley's Symptoms

ASHLEY HAS BEEN A MEMBER of some of the internet groups for a number of years. Through various types of treatments he is now much better.

Ashley went for help very late after his symptoms began to appear. As he put it, "By the time it really sunk in there was something seriously wrong with me, I was a hell of a mess. I wish the people at my job has mentioned something to me instead of just forcing me out."

The list Ashley has kindly allowed me to reproduce is the one he made up for his psychiatrist. Not everyone is going to be this bad.

Ashley's diagnosis was severe clinical depression and very high generalized anxiety disorder.

Now that you have been through the book, the symptoms should be more meaningful to you than if they were placed on page one as an attention getter.

- can't deal with anything
- can't go near my work place or talk to people about it

- can't make decisions
- can't offer support to my wife who is ill
- can't speak up when shortchanged, wrong item, etc.
- depressed
- dizzy
- don't want to answer phone
- don't want to look at mail
- during a very stressful situation which I have to handle, I feel like I am tucked away in the back of my head while a small part of me continues to carry on. It is like I am standing back watching and listening to myself
- ear ringing
- eczema—never had it before
- feel a deep deep tiredness
- feel like an old worn-out man
- feel like hands swelling to a huge size
- filling out forms: after a few minutes I can't understand them—then become very tired and shaky for days
- flustered very easily to the point of immobility
- forget where I am going
- forget what I am doing
- "freeze" when asked unexpected questions
- "freeze" when under the slightest stress
- had to start using inhalator when stressed
- hands developed sensory hallucinations
- hands numb
- have to "escape" when surrounded by more than a few people
- hands shake

- have to stay out of stressful situations
- heart beats fast
- I turn out garbage but it seems OK at the time I write it
- if experiencing slightest stress—start shaking
- just want to be left alone
- loss of bowel and bladder control
- many old allergies returning
- mind goes blank when looking at lesson plan in front of class
- mind goes blank when under stress
- new allergies
- panting
- sleep a great deal, particularly after a stressful day (12 to 15 hours)
- stomach cramps
- sweat when under the slightest emotional stress
- takes days for me to fill out even short forms—then laid out for 2 or 3 days
- takes hours to write a short letter
- tension headaches
- tension level was so high it was up to "my eyeballs" last September
- unable to think clearly
- unexpected events make me freeze
- very snappy
- wake up paralyzed for up to 43 breaths

Some time later I had a CHAT room discussion with Ashley. Short sections of the discussion on the internet are given below.

Ken: How are you feeling now, Ashley?

Ashley: Much better thanks. It took a few years and a lot of support but I am now able to work again.

Ken: Are you going back to the same place?

Ashley: No way! They treated me terribly there.

Ken: Can you talk about it? You don't have to.

Ashley: That is OK. I have learned to deal with it now.

Ken: What were they doing?

Ashley: As you know depression creeps up on you and you don't know what is wrong. I felt things were not right but I could not put my finger on it. Turns out I was not doing a very good job. After 23 years my work started to slip. Surely they must have known something was wrong.

Ken: Did they speak to you about it?

Ashley: No, that is not the way they operate. Once it was obvious I was not doing a good job they started to make things worse. Middle management made comments about me to others making sure it came back to me. The management also had loaded me up with impossible assignments. The stress and worry just compounded it all until I could not work any longer.

Ken: So did you quit?

Ashley: I almost did but I contacted my union and they told me not to quit but to take sick leave. Once I got on sick leave I found there was help available. But then I was not dealing with other people. And by not quitting I was eligible for medical help and counseling as well as other types of financial help.

Ken: Do you know why middle management did nothing to help you?

Ashley: After 23 years I had a great deal of seniority. Middle management just wanted to get rid of me in any way they could. As a person I no longer counted.

Ken: Regrettably I have seen it before, Ashley. As a department. head I saw people in my department who had reached some type of burnout be treated in that way. I did not endear myself to management by interceding but little was ever done to me for doing it.

Ashley: I have discovered it is not uncommon.

Ken: So now you move on?

Ashley: I guess I should put it behind me but my lawyer says I can probably sue for the way they treated me. I also hear there is now legislation in place which prevents people from being laid off solely due to illness including so called "mental."

Ken: Yes there is. Progress has been made in that area but there is still much educating to do.

Thanks, Ashley, for allowing me to use that. I am sure the severe symptoms you showed and the treatment given to you by your long-term employer will open other people's eyes.

Twenty-two

How I Got Over My Panic Attacks and Agoraphobia

IT IS ONLY NORMAL FOR PEOPLE with anxiety to ask others how they got over it. This is a question I have been asked many times. I answer to the best of my ability but caution them that it is only me...everyone is different. Also, keep in mind that 30 years ago anxiety and panic attacks were very poorly understood and many professionals were really not acquainted with them.

In about 1973 I was diagnosed with cancer. It was a five-year battle to get over it. Along the line several things happened. One of them occurred about the end of the fourth year. I began to shake, sweat, disassociate and develop several other scary symptoms. I mentioned them at the cancer clinic and was told it was probably the drugs they were giving me, and they would disappear once I completed taking the medications. They also told me the weird symptoms were not harmful.

Therefore, I had been given a reason for the strange attacks and I had been told there was an end point. With this information I plowed ahead doing my best until such a time as the effects from the drugs wore off. The symptoms did not stop but kept on almost getting worse.

Fast-forward to several months after treatment and the attacks had not stopped. Rather than being scared I was mad that they had not gone away as advertised. I am sure it helped considerably that my university studies emphasized human biology and psychology. I approached the situation as a puzzle. First question was what was going on inside of me. The next was why. Again it helped that I have always been able to stand back and look at my body's reactions to things without being too much of a part of it.

I really don't recall if I went so far as to relate to a fight or flight condition but I was able to recognize the reasons behind many of the strange symptoms. Knowing what was going on inside of me helped dramatically. I was no longer afraid of the feelings. In fact I would joke with myself and say that people paid good money for street drugs just to feel this way. On top of that, excuse the expression, I was becoming very pissed off that the attacks didn't go away. I didn't realize it at the time but, by not being afraid, I had destroyed the positive feedback loop that makes them grow. I then started looking for the triggers. In my case most were external, such as the large black and white checker board squares of a department store in town; in a busy restaurant the food in my throat made me feel like I choking and off we went again. When the triggers had been identified I was no longer surprised when the panic attacks hit. (Oh, yes, along the line I was given some tranquilizers. Diazapam was big at that time.)

Shortly after I adopted my approach to the attacks they began to fade and no longer bothered me as much. In time they left but even now from time to time I can still feel a twinge of one starting up but they never amount to much.

I emphasize that I was not being particularly brilliant or being blessed with any special insight...I just learned to approach them with an air of curiosity, not fear.

The agoraphobia didn't seem to want to leave either. I have mentioned earlier in this book that the difficulty I had trying to leave the property was not due to a conscious fear of panic attacks. It was more like trying to push two north poles of a magnet together with the property line being one north pole and me being the other. Again, I was blessed with being able to take the approach of curiosity rather than fear. Here was a strange phenomenon. What is going on and do I ever get over it? Never did answer the first question but I did get over it.

There are many suggestions in this book on how to work on the agoraphobia. My method was really just to push the envelope a bit more each time. If I couldn't drive past the end of the street, OK, I would stop there and relax. If I calmed down I might go further or just turn around depending upon how I felt. The next time I would go a little further, etc. I know this method does not work for everyone, but it did for me. Remember the method that worked for me is not necessarily for everyone but I am a great believer in feeling a person has less of a rough time with panic attacks and agoraphobia if they understand what is going on and accept it is not going to kill you. That is one reason I have placed the symptoms and causes of the symptoms on page 27.

After reading the above I realize I have given a very simplistic account of my time with the disorders. I have not mentioned them striking out of the blue nor the times I had to hang onto the chalk ledge in my classroom and carry on with the lesson with none of the students aware anything was wrong. Also, one thing which has just hit me—I had stumbled onto a few of the methods of treatment that are now widely used, *i.e.,* exposure therapy, cognitive behavioral therapy and medications.

Twenty-three

Signs for Around the Home

MANY PEOPLE HAVE FOUND it helpful to post signs around the house to remind them to discourage certain thoughts, enforce attitudes, control responses, etc.

Here are a few suggestions.

 **Thoughts**

- I don't have to answer the phone.
- Am I catastophizing?
- Breathe slowly.
- All is well.
- So what!

- Is that really important?
- I don't have to have an answer right now.
- Stop! Think!
- Does it really matter?
- No big deal.
- It's not important so don't sweat it.
- The subconscious is non-judgemental. Feed your mind good thoughts and images about yourself and soon your mind will be sending them back to you.

These Thoughts Are Not Permitted

- I should have
- If only
- What if
- I screwed up again.
- It's always my fault.

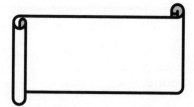

Good Thoughts

- I count.
- I respect myself.
- I have great potential.
- I can face my anxieties and work to overcome them.

Twenty-four

Resources Mentioned in the Text
(and a Few Others)

"...nine, ten, do it again. A Guide to Obsessive Compulsive Disorder. For People with OCD & Their Families"
A comprehensive straight talking book by, Kathryn l'Anson, director of the Anxiety Recovery Center, Victoria, Australia. The ISBN is 0-646-30807-6

The Panic Anxiety Hub
One of the top sites in Australia. It is run by the well-known Bronwyn Fox who lectures, gives courses and has written several book on panic and anxiety. Some of the courses are also available online. Information is available on www.panicattacks.com.au

Anxiety Disorders Unit. University of British Columbia, Vancouver, B.C., Canada
The ADABC is a nonprofit society formed to increase awareness of anxiety disorders and currently available treatments. Sarah Newth is the provincial liaison person for anxiety. www.anxietybc.com/

Panic Disorders Institute. Pasadena, California
Dr. Stuart Shipco may be reached through www.algy.com/pdi/

Dr. Ian Gillespie
Psychiatrist. Victoria, B.C., Canada. Dr. Gillespie's site is dedicated to providing information about driving safety to physicians, drivers and their families. www.drivesafe.com

Dr. David Perry
Psychologist. University of Westminster. London, England. http://users.wmin.ac.uk/~stonesa/paq/paq.htm

Dr. Andjelka Stones-Abbasi
Psychologist formerly with the University of Westminster, London, England and now co-founder of the Global Egg Donation Resource which was established with a goal of providing the most accurate and the most honest information possible to those seeking egg donation treatment as well as establishing a GLOBAL collaboration of all professionals working in this field. http://www.gedr.com/

tAPir —The Panic Anxiety Information Resource
One of the most comprehensive resources on the web for anxiety disorders. Links include, CHAT groups, information sites, medication, support group locations throughout the world...just to mention a few. http://www.algy.com/anxiety/menu.shtml

Anxiety Disorders—The Caregiver
This site is my own. It is recognized as probably the premier site on the web for support people to those anxiety disorders. http://pacificcoast.net/~kstrong/

There are also a number of mail lists associated with the site.

For support people and those with anxiety who wish seek support, trade information, etc. To join this group send a blank email to ACSL-subscribe@yahoo groups.com

To join a mail list for support people only, send a blank email to anxietydisorders-thecaregivers-subscribe @yahoogroups.com

There are a couple of other anxiety mail lists you may wish to consider. They are primarily for those with anxiety disorders:

Anxiety-A-subscribe@yahoogroups.com and Anxiety-L-subscribe@yahoogroups.com

Healthy Place
A site which offers information, live discussions and CHAT groups for many mental disorders. The home page is http://healthyplace.com/index.html

From there you can get into any of the "communities" on the site.

Panic Center
This site offers on line tests for panic, resources and a free on line program based upon cognitive behavioral therapy. Definitely worth visiting. www.paniccenter.net

National Institute of Mental Health
Loaded with up to date information on mental health and disorders. http://www.nimh.nih.gov/

Chat Group
One of my favorite Chat Groups can be located through http://anxietyneighborhood.dune.net/

Mental Health Strategies

The Government of British Columbia has recently released strategies on dealing with anxiety and depression. Since they have just been released (at the time of writing) I presume they are the most up to date techniques available.

Anxiety: www.healthservices.gov.bc.ca/mhd/pdf/anxietystrategy.pdf

Depression: www.healthservices.gov.bc.ca/mhd/pdf/depressionstrategy.pdf